AI
Self-Driving Cars
Autonomy

Practical Advances in
Artificial Intelligence and Machine Learning

Dr. Lance B. Eliot, MBA, PhD

DEDICATION

To my incredible daughter, Lauren, and my incredible son, Michael.

Forest fortuna adiuvat (from the Latin; good fortune favors the brave).

CONTENTS

Lance B. Eliot

ACKNOWLEDGMENTS

I have been the beneficiary of advice and counsel by many friends, colleagues, family, investors, and many others. I want to thank everyone that has aided me throughout my career. I write from the heart and the head, having experienced first-hand what it means to have others around you that support you during the good times and the tough times.

To Warren Bennis, one of my doctoral advisors and ultimately a colleague, I offer my deepest thanks and appreciation, especially for his calm and insightful wisdom and support.

To Mark Stevens and his generous efforts toward funding and supporting the USC Stevens Center for Innovation.

To Lloyd Greif and the USC Lloyd Greif Center for Entrepreneurial Studies for their ongoing encouragement of founders and entrepreneurs.

To Peter Drucker, William Wang, Aaron Levie, Peter Kim, Jon Kraft, Cindy Crawford, Jenny Ming, Steve Milligan, Chis Underwood, Frank Gehry, Buzz Aldrin, Steve Forbes, Bill Thompson, Dave Dillon, Alan Fuerstman, Larry Ellison, Jim Sinegal, John Sperling, Mark Stevenson, Anand Nallathambi, Thomas Barrack, Jr., and many other innovators and leaders that I have met and gained mightily from doing so.

Thanks to Ed Trainor, Kevin Anderson, James Hickey, Wendell Jones, Ken Harris, DuWayne Peterson, Mike Brown, Jim Thornton, Abhi Beniwal, Al Biland, John Nomura, Eliot Weinman, John Desmond, and many others for their unwavering support during my career.

And most of all thanks as always to Lauren and Michael, for their ongoing support and for having seen me writing and heard much of this material during the many months involved in writing it. To their patience and willingness to listen.

Lance B. Eliot

INTRODUCTION

This is a book that provides the newest innovations and the latest Artificial Intelligence (AI) advances about the emerging nature of AI-based autonomous self-driving driverless cars. Via recent advances in Artificial Intelligence (AI) and Machine Learning (ML), we are nearing the day when vehicles can control themselves and will not require and nor rely upon human intervention to perform their driving tasks (or, that <u>allow</u> for human intervention, but only *require* human intervention in very limited ways).

Similar to my other related books, which I describe in a moment and list the chapters in the Appendix A of this book, I am particularly focused on those advances that pertain to self-driving cars. The phrase "autonomous vehicles" is often used to refer to any kind of vehicle, whether it is ground-based or in the air or sea, and whether it is a cargo hauling trailer truck or a conventional passenger car. Though the aspects described in this book are certainly applicable to all kinds of autonomous vehicles, I am focused more so here on cars.

Indeed, I am especially known for my role in aiding the advancement of self-driving cars, serving currently as the Executive Director of the Cybernetic AI Self-Driving Cars Institute. In addition to writing software, designing and developing systems and software for self-driving cars, I also speak and write quite a bit about the topic. This book is a collection of some of my more advanced essays. For those of you that might have seen my essays posted elsewhere, I have updated them and integrated them into this book as one handy cohesive package.

You might be interested in companion books that I have written that provide additional key innovations and fundamentals about self-driving cars. Those books are entitled **"Introduction to Driverless Self-Driving Cars," "Advances in AI and Autonomous Vehicles: Cybernetic Self-Driving Cars," "Self-Driving Cars: "The Mother of All AI Projects," "Innovation and Thought Leadership on Self-Driving Driverless Cars," "New Advances in AI Autonomous Driverless Self-Driving Cars," "Autonomous Vehicle Driverless Self-Driving Cars and Artificial Intelligence," "Transformative Artificial Intelligence**

Driverless Self-Driving Cars," "Disruptive Artificial Intelligence and Driverless Self-Driving Cars, and "State-of-the-Art AI Driverless Self-Driving Cars," and "Top Trends in AI Self-Driving Cars," and "AI Innovations and Self-Driving Cars," "Crucial Advances for AI Driverless Cars," "Sociotechnical Insights and AI Driverless Cars," "Pioneering Advances for AI Driverless Cars" and "Leading Edge Trends for AI Driverless Cars," "The Cutting Edge of AI Autonomous Cars" and "The Next Wave of AI Self-Driving Cars" and "Revolutionary Innovations of AI Self-Driving Cars," and "AI Self-Driving Cars Breakthroughs," "Trailblazing Trends for AI Self-Driving Cars," "Ingenious Strides for AI Driverless Cars," "AI Self-Driving Cars Inventiveness," "Visionary Secrets of AI Driverless Cars," "Spearheading AI Self-Driving Cars," "Spurring AI Self-Driving Cars," "Avant-Garde AI Driverless Cars," "AI Self-Driving Cars Evolvement," "AI Driverless Cars Chrysalis," "Boosting AI Autonomous Cars," "AI Self-Driving Cars Trendsetting," "AI Autonomous Cars Forefront, "AI Autonomous Cars Emergence," "AI Autonomous Cars Progress," "AI Self-Driving Cars Prognosis," "AI Self-Driving Cars Momentum," "AI Self-Driving Cars Headway," "AI Self-Driving Cars Vicissitude," "AI Self-Driving Cars Autonomy" (they are available on Amazon).

For this book, I am going to borrow my introduction from those companion books, since it does a good job of laying out the landscape of self-driving cars and my overall viewpoints on the topic. The remainder of this book is material that does not appear in the companion books.

INTRODUCTION TO SELF-DRIVING CARS

This is a book about self-driving cars. Someday in the future, we'll all have self-driving cars and this book will perhaps seem antiquated, but right now, we are at the forefront of the self-driving car wave. Daily news bombards us with flashes of new announcements by one car maker or another and leaves the impression that within the next few weeks or maybe months that the self-driving car will be here. A casual non-technical reader would assume from these news flashes that in fact we must be on the cusp of a true self-driving car. We are still quite a distance from having a true self-driving car.

A true self-driving car is akin to a moonshot. In the same manner that getting us to the moon was an incredible feat, likewise, is achieving a true self-driving car. Anybody that suggests or even brashly states that the true self-driving car is nearly here should be viewed with great skepticism. Indeed, you'll see that I often tend to use the word "hogwash" or "crock" when I assess much of the decidedly *fake news* about self-driving cars.

Indeed, I've been writing a popular blog post about self-driving cars and hitting hard on those that try to wave their hands and pretend that we are on the imminent verge of true self-driving cars. For many years, I've been known as the AI Insider. Besides writing about AI, I also develop AI software. I do what I describe. It also gives me insights into what others that are doing AI are really doing versus what it is said they are doing.

Many faithful readers had asked me to pull together my insightful short essays and put them into another book, which you are now holding.

For those of you that have been reading my essays over the years, this collection not only puts them together into one handy package, I also updated the essays and added new material. For those of you that are new to the topic of self-driving cars and AI, I hope you find these essays approachable and informative. I also tend to have a writing style with a bit of a voice, and so you'll see that I am times have a wry sense of humor and poke at conformity.

As a former professor and founder of an AI research lab, I for many years wrote in the formal language of academic writing. I published in referred journals and served as an editor for several AI journals. This writing here is not of the nature, and I have adopted a different and more informal style for these essays. That being said, I also do mention from time-to-time more rigorous material on AI and encourage you all to dig into those deeper and more formal materials if so interested.

I am also an AI practitioner. This means that I write AI software for a living. Currently, I head-up the Cybernetics Self-Driving Car Institute, where we are developing AI software for self-driving cars.

For those of you that are reading this book and have a penchant for writing code, you might consider taking a look at the open source code available for self-driving cars. This is a handy place to start learning how to develop AI for self-driving cars. There are also many new educational courses spring forth. There is a growing body of those wanting to learn about and develop self-driving cars, and a growing body of colleges, labs, and other avenues by which you can learn about self-driving cars.

This book will provide a foundation of aspects that I think will get you ready for those kinds of more advanced training opportunities. If you've already taken those classes, you'll likely find these essays especially interesting as they offer a perspective that I am betting few other instructors or faculty offered to you. These are challenging essays that ask you to think beyond the conventional about self-driving cars.

THE MOTHER OF ALL AI PROJECTS

In June 2017, Apple CEO Tim Cook came out and finally admitted that Apple has been working on a self-driving car. As you'll see in my essays, Apple was enmeshed in secrecy about their self-driving car efforts. We have only been able to read the tea leaves and guess at what Apple has been up to. The notion of an iCar has been floating for quite a while, and self-driving engineers and researchers have been signing tight-lipped Non-Disclosure Agreements (NDA's) to work on projects at Apple that were as shrouded in mystery as any military invasion plans might be.

Tim Cook said something that many others in the Artificial Intelligence (AI) field have been saying, namely, the creation of a self-driving car has got to be the mother of all AI projects. In other words, it is in fact a tremendous moonshot for AI. If a self-driving car can be crafted and the AI works as we hope, it means that we have made incredible strides with AI and that therefore it opens many other worlds of potential breakthrough accomplishments that AI can solve.

Is this hyperbole? Am I just trying to make AI seem like a miracle worker and so provide self-aggrandizing statements for those of us writing the AI software for self-driving cars? No, it is not hyperbole. Developing a true self-driving car is really, really, really hard to do. Let me take a moment to explain why. As a side note, I realize that the Apple CEO is known for at times uttering hyperbole, and he had previously said for example that the year 2012 was "the mother of all years," and he had said that the release of iOS 10 was "the mother of all releases" – all of which does suggest he likes to use the handy "mother of" expression. But, I assure you, in terms of true self-driving cars, he has hit the nail on the head. For sure.

When you think about a moonshot and how we got to the moon, there are some identifiable characteristics and those same aspects can be applied to creating a true self-driving car. You'll notice that I keep putting the word "true" in front of the self-driving car expression. I do so because as per my essay about the various levels of self-driving cars, there are some self-driving cars that are only somewhat of a self-driving car. The somewhat versions are ones that require a human driver to be ready to intervene. In my view, that's not a true self-driving car. A true self-driving car is one that requires no human driver intervention at all. It is a car that can entirely undertake via automation the driving task without any human driver needed. This is the essence of what is known as a Level 5 self-driving car. We are currently at the Level 2 and Level 3 mark, and not yet at Level 5.

Getting to the moon involved aspects such as having big stretch goals, incremental progress, experimentation, innovation, and so on. Let's review how this applied to the moonshot of the bygone era, and how it applies to the self-driving car moonshot of today.

Big Stretch Goal

Trying to take a human and deliver the human to the moon, and bring them back, safely, was an extremely large stretch goal at the time. No one knew whether it could be done. The technology wasn't available yet. The cost was huge. The determination would need to be fierce. Etc. To reach a Level 5 self-driving car is going to be the same. It is a big stretch goal. We can readily get to the Level 3, and we are able to see the Level 4 just up ahead, but a Level 5 is still an unknown as to if it is doable. It should eventually be doable and in the same way that we thought we'd eventually get to the moon, but when it will occur is a different story.

Incremental Progress

Getting to the moon did not happen overnight in one fell swoop. It took years and years of incremental progress to get there. Likewise for self-driving cars. Google has famously been striving to get to the Level 5, and pretty much been willing to forgo dealing with the intervening levels, but most of the other self-driving car makers are doing the incremental route. Let's get a good Level 2 and a somewhat Level 3 going. Then, let's improve the Level 3 and get a somewhat Level 4 going. Then, let's improve the Level 4 and finally arrive at a Level 5. This seems to be the prevalent way that we are going to achieve the true self-driving car.

Experimentation

You likely know that there were various experiments involved in perfecting the approach and technology to get to the moon. As per making incremental progress, we first tried to see if we could get a rocket to go into space and safety return, then put a monkey in there, then with a human, then we went all the way to the moon but didn't land, and finally we arrived at the mission that actually landed on the moon. Self-driving cars are the same way. We are doing simulations of self-driving cars. We do testing of self-driving cars on private land under controlled situations. We do testing of self-driving cars on public roadways, often having to meet regulatory requirements including for example having an engineer or equivalent in the car to take over the controls if needed. And so on. Experiments big and small are needed to figure out what works and what doesn't.

Innovation

There are already some advances in AI that are allowing us to progress toward self-driving cars. We are going to need even more advances. Innovation in all aspects of technology are going to be required to achieve a true self-driving car. By no means do we already have everything in-hand that we need to get there. Expect new inventions and new approaches, new algorithms, etc.

Setbacks

Most of the pundits are avoiding talking about potential setbacks in the progress toward self-driving cars. Getting to the moon involved many setbacks, some of which you never have heard of and were buried at the time so as to not dampen enthusiasm and funding for getting to the moon. A recurring theme in many of my included essays is that there are going to be setbacks as we try to arrive at a true self-driving car. Take a deep breath and be ready. I just hope the setbacks don't completely stop progress. I am sure that it will cause progress to alter in a manner that we've not yet seen in the self-driving car field. I liken the self-driving car of today to the excitement everyone had for Uber when it first got going. Today, we have a different view of Uber and with each passing day there are more regulations to the ride sharing business and more concerns raised. The darling child only stays a darling until finally that child acts up. It will happen the same with self-driving cars.

SELF-DRIVING CARS CHALLENGES

But what exactly makes things so hard to have a true self-driving car, you might be asking. You have seen cruise control for years and years. You've lately seen cars that can do parallel parking. You've seen YouTube videos of Tesla drivers that put their hands out the window as their car zooms along the highway, and seen to therefore be in a self-driving car. Aren't we just needing to put a few more sensors onto a car and then we'll have in-hand a true self-driving car? Nope.

Consider for a moment the nature of the driving task. We don't just let anyone at any age drive a car. Worldwide, most countries won't license a driver until the age of 18, though many do allow a learner's permit at the age of 15 or 16. Some suggest that a younger age would be physically too small to reach the controls of the car. Though this might be the case, we could easily adjust the controls to allow for younger aged and thus smaller stature.

It's not their physical size that matters. It's their cognitive development that matters.

To drive a car, you need to be able to reason about the car, what the car can and cannot do. You need to know how to operate the car. You need to know about how other cars on the road drive. You need to know what is allowed in driving such as speed limits and driving within marked lanes. You need to be able to react to situations and be able to avoid getting into accidents. You need to ascertain when to hit your brakes, when to steer clear of a pedestrian, and how to keep from ramming that motorcyclist that just cut you off.

Many of us had taken courses on driving. We studied about driving and took driver training. We had to take a test and pass it to be able to drive. The point being that though most adults take the driving task for granted, and we often "mindlessly" drive our cars, there is a significant amount of cognitive effort that goes into driving a car. After a while, it becomes second nature. You don't especially think about how you drive, you just do it. But, if you watch a novice driver, say a teenager learning to drive, you suddenly realize that there is a lot more complexity to it than we seem to realize.

Furthermore, driving is a very serious task. I recall when my daughter and son first learned to drive. They are both very conscientious people. They wanted to make sure that whatever they did, they did well, and that they did not harm anyone. Every day, when you get into a car, it is probably around 4,000 pounds of hefty metal and plastics (about two tons), and it is a lethal weapon. Think about it. You drive down the street in an object that weighs two tons and with the engine it can accelerate and ram into anything you want to hit. The damage a car can inflict is very scary. Both my children were surprised that they were being given the right to maneuver this monster of a beast that could cause tremendous harm entirely by merely letting go of the steering wheel for a moment or taking your eyes off the road.

In fact, in the United States alone there are about 30,000 deaths per year by auto accidents, which is around 100 per day. Given that there are about 263 million cars in the United States, I am actually more amazed that the number of fatalities is not a lot higher. During my morning commute, I look at all the thousands of cars on the freeway around me, and I think that if all of them decided to go zombie and drive in a crazy maniac way, there would be many people dead. Somehow, incredibly, each day, most people drive relatively safely. To me, that's a miracle right there. Getting millions and millions of people to be safe and sane when behind the wheel of a two ton mobile object, it's a feat that we as a society should admire with pride.

So, hopefully you are in agreement that the driving task requires a great deal of cognition. You don't' need to be especially smart to drive a car, and we've done quite a bit to make car driving viable for even the average dolt. There isn't an IQ test that you need to take to drive a car. If you can read and write, and pass a test, you pretty much can legally drive a car. There are of course some that drive a car and are not legally permitted to do so, plus there are private areas such as farms where drivers are young, but for public roadways in the United States, you can be generally of average intelligence (or less) and be able to legally drive.

This though makes it seem like the cognitive effort must not be much. If the cognitive effort was truly hard, wouldn't we only have Einstein's that could drive a car? We have made sure to keep the driving task as simple as we can, by making the controls easy and relatively standardized, and by having roads that are relatively standardized, and so on. It is as though Disneyland has put their Autopia into the real-world, by us all as a society agreeing that roads will be a certain way, and we'll all abide by the various rules of driving.

A modest cognitive task by a human is still something that stymies AI. You certainly know that AI has been able to beat chess players and be good at other kinds of games. This type of narrow cognition is not what car driving is about. Car driving is much wider. It requires knowledge about the world, which a chess playing AI system does not need to know. The cognitive aspects of driving are on the one hand seemingly simple, but at the same time require layer upon layer of knowledge about cars, people, roads, rules, and a myriad of other "common sense" aspects. We don't have any AI systems today that have that same kind of breadth and depth of awareness and knowledge.

As revealed in my essays, the self-driving car of today is using trickery to do particular tasks. It is all very narrow in operation. Plus, it currently assumes that a human driver is ready to intervene. It is like a child that we have taught to stack blocks, but we are needed to be right there in case the child stacks them too high and they begin to fall over. AI of today is brittle, it is narrow, and it does not approach the cognitive abilities of humans. This is why the true self-driving car is somewhere out in the future.

Another aspect to the driving task is that it is not solely a mind exercise. You do need to use your senses to drive. You use your eyes a vision sensors to see the road ahead. You vision capability is like a streaming video, which your brain needs to continually analyze as you drive. Where is the road? Is there a pedestrian in the way? Is there another car ahead of you? Your senses are relying a flood of info to your brain. Self-driving cars are trying to do the same, by using cameras, radar, ultrasound, and lasers. This is an attempt at mimicking how humans have senses and sensory apparatus.

Thus, the driving task is mental and physical. You use your senses, you use your arms and legs to manipulate the controls of the car, and you use your brain to assess the sensory info and direct your limbs to act upon the controls of the car. This all happens instantly. If you've ever perhaps gotten something in your eye and only had one eye available to drive with, you suddenly realize how dependent upon vision you are. If you have a broken foot with a cast, you suddenly realize how hard it is to control the brake pedal and the accelerator. If you've taken medication and your brain is maybe sluggish, you suddenly realize how much mental strain is required to drive a car.

An AI system that plays chess only needs to be focused on playing chess. The physical aspects aren't important because usually a human moves the chess pieces or the chessboard is shown on an electronic display. Using AI for a more life-and-death task such as analyzing MRI images of patients, this again does not require physical capabilities and instead is done by examining images of bits.

Driving a car is a true life-and-death task. It is a use of AI that can easily and at any moment produce death. For those colleagues of mine that are developing this AI, as am I, we need to keep in mind the somber aspects of this. We are producing software that will have in its virtual hands the lives of the occupants of the car, and the lives of those in other nearby cars, and the lives of nearby pedestrians, etc. Chess is not usually a life-or-death matter.

Driving is all around us. Cars are everywhere. Most of today's AI applications involve only a small number of people. Or, they are behind the scenes and we as humans have other recourse if the AI messes up. AI that is driving a car at 80 miles per hour on a highway had better not mess up. The consequences are grave. Multiply this by the number of cars, if we could put magically self-driving into every car in the USA, we'd have AI running in the 263 million cars. That's a lot of AI spread around. This is AI on a massive scale that we are not doing today and that offers both promise and potential peril.

There are some that want AI for self-driving cars because they envision a world without any car accidents. They envision a world in which there is no car congestion and all cars cooperate with each other. These are wonderful utopian visions.

They are also very misleading. The adoption of self-driving cars is going to be incremental and not overnight. We cannot economically just junk all existing cars. Nor are we going to be able to affordably retrofit existing cars. It is more likely that self-driving cars will be built into new cars and that over many years of gradual replacement of existing cars that we'll see the mix of self-driving cars become substantial in the real-world.

In these essays, I have tried to offer technological insights without being overly technical in my description, and also blended the business, societal, and economic aspects too. Technologists need to consider the non-technological impacts of what they do. Non-technologists should be aware of what is being developed.

We all need to work together to collectively be prepared for the enormous disruption and transformative aspects of true self-driving cars. We all need to be involved in this mother of all AI projects.

WHAT THIS BOOK PROVIDES

What does this book provide to you? It introduces many of the key elements about self-driving cars and does so with an AI based perspective. I weave together technical and non-technical aspects, readily going from being concerned about the cognitive capabilities of the driving task and how the technology is embodying this into self-driving cars, and in the next breath I discuss the societal and economic aspects.

They are all intertwined because that's the way reality is. You cannot separate out the technology per se, and instead must consider it within the milieu of what is being invented and innovated, and do so with a mindset towards the contemporary mores and culture that shape what we are doing and what we hope to do.

WHY THIS BOOK

I wrote this book to try and bring to the public view many aspects about self-driving cars that nobody seems to be discussing.

For business leaders that are either involved in making self-driving cars or that are going to leverage self-driving cars, I hope that this book will enlighten you as to the risks involved and ways in which you should be strategizing about how to deal with those risks.

For entrepreneurs, startups and other businesses that want to enter into the self-driving car market that is emerging, I hope this book sparks your interest in doing so, and provides some sense of what might be prudent to pursue.

For researchers that study self-driving cars, I hope this book spurs your interest in the risks and safety issues of self-driving cars, and also nudges you toward conducting research on those aspects.

For students in computer science or related disciplines, I hope this book will provide you with interesting and new ideas and material, for which you might conduct research or provide some career direction insights for you.

For AI companies and high-tech companies pursuing self-driving cars, this book will hopefully broaden your view beyond just the mere coding and development needed to make self-driving cars.

For all readers, I hope that you will find the material in this book to be stimulating. Some of it will be repetitive of things you already know. But I am pretty sure that you'll also find various eureka moments whereby you'll discover a new technique or approach that you had not earlier thought of. I am also betting that there will be material that forces you to rethink some of your current practices.

I am not saying you will suddenly have an epiphany and change what you are doing. I do think though that you will reconsider or perhaps revisit what you are doing.

For anyone choosing to use this book for teaching purposes, please take a look at my suggestions for doing so, as described in the Appendix. I have found the material handy in courses that I have taught, and likewise other faculty have told me that they have found the material handy, in some cases as extended readings and in other instances as a core part of their course (depending on the nature of the class).

In my writing for this book, I have tried carefully to blend both the practitioner and the academic styles of writing. It is not as dense as is typical academic journal writing, but at the same time offers depth by going into the nuances and trade-offs of various practices.

The word "deep" is in vogue today, meaning getting deeply into a subject or topic, and so is the word "unpack" which means to tease out the underlying aspects of a subject or topic. I have sought to offer material that addresses an issue or topic by going relatively deeply into it and make sure that it is well unpacked.

In any book about AI, it is difficult to use our everyday words without having some of them be misinterpreted. Specifically, it is easy to anthropomorphize AI. When I say that an AI system "knows" something, I do not want you to construe that the AI system has sentience and "knows" in the same way that humans do. They aren't that way, as yet. I have tried to use quotes around such words from time-to-time to emphasize that the words I am using should not be misinterpreted to ascribe true human intelligence to the AI systems that we know of today. If I used quotes around all such words, the book would be very difficult to read, and so I am doing so judiciously. Please keep that in mind as you read the material, thanks.

Some of the material is time-based in terms of covering underway activities, and though some of it might decay, nonetheless I believe you'll find the material useful and informative.

COMPANION BOOKS

1. **"Introduction to Driverless Self-Driving Cars"** by Dr. Lance Eliot
2. **"Innovation and Thought Leadership on Self-Driving Driverless Cars"** by Dr. Lance Eliot
3. **"Advances in AI and Autonomous Vehicles: Cybernetic Self-Driving Cars"** by Dr. Lance Eliot
4. **"Self-Driving Cars: The Mother of All AI Projects"** by Dr. Lance Eliot
5. **"New Advances in AI Autonomous Driverless Self-Driving Cars"** by Dr. Lance Eliot
6. **"Autonomous Vehicle Driverless Self-Driving Cars and Artificial Intelligence"** by Dr. Lance Eliot and Michael B. Eliot
7. **"Transformative Artificial Intelligence Driverless Self-Driving Cars"** by Dr. Lance Eliot
8. **"Disruptive Artificial Intelligence and Driverless Self-Driving Cars"** by Dr. Lance Eliot
9. "State-of-the-Art AI Driverless Self-Driving Cars" by Dr. Lance Eliot
10. "Top Trends in AI Self-Driving Cars" by Dr. Lance Eliot
11. **"AI Innovations and Self-Driving Cars"** by Dr. Lance Eliot
12. **"Crucial Advances for AI Driverless Cars"** by Dr. Lance Eliot
13. **"Sociotechnical Insights and AI Driverless Cars"** by Dr. Lance Eliot.
14. **"Pioneering Advances for AI Driverless Cars"** by Dr. Lance Eliot
15. **"Leading Edge Trends for AI Driverless Cars"** by Dr. Lance Eliot
16. **"The Cutting Edge of AI Autonomous Cars"** by Dr. Lance Eliot
17. **"The Next Wave of AI Self-Driving Cars"** by Dr. Lance Eliot
18. **"Revolutionary Innovations of AI Driverless Cars"** by Dr. Lance Eliot
19. **"AI Self-Driving Cars Breakthroughs"** by Dr. Lance Eliot
20. **"Trailblazing Trends for AI Self-Driving Cars"** by Dr. Lance Eliot
21. **"Ingenious Strides for AI Driverless Cars"** by Dr. Lance Eliot
22. **"AI Self-Driving Cars Inventiveness"** by Dr. Lance Eliot
23. **"Visionary Secrets of AI Driverless Cars"** by Dr. Lance Eliot
24. **"Spearheading AI Self-Driving Cars"** by Dr. Lance Eliot
25. **"Spurring AI Self-Driving Cars"** by Dr. Lance Eliot
26. **"Avant-Garde AI Driverless Cars"** by Dr. Lance Eliot
27. **"AI Self-Driving Cars Evolvement"** by Dr. Lance Eliot
28. **"AI Driverless Cars Chrysalis"** by Dr. Lance Eliot
29. **"Boosting AI Autonomous Cars"** by Dr. Lance Eliot
30. **"AI Self-Driving Cars Trendsetting"** by Dr. Lance Eliot
31. **"AI Autonomous Cars Forefront"** by Dr. Lance Eliot
32. **"AI Autonomous Cars Emergence"** by Dr. Lance Eliot
33. **"AI Autonomous Cars Progress"** by Dr. Lance Eliot
34. **"AI Self-Driving Cars Prognosis"** by Dr. Lance Eliot
35. **"AI Self-Driving Cars Momentum"** by Dr. Lance Eliot
36. **"AI Self-Driving Cars Headway"** by Dr. Lance Eliot
37. **"AI Self-Driving Cars Vicissitude"** by Dr. Lance Eliot
38. **"AI Self-Driving Cars Autonomy"** by Dr. Lance Eliot

These books are available on Amazon and at other major global booksellers.

CHAPTER 1

ELIOT FRAMEWORK FOR AI SELF-DRIVING CARS

CHAPTER 1

ELIOT FRAMEWORK FOR
AI SELF-DRIVING CARS

This chapter is a core foundational aspect for understanding AI self-driving cars and I have used this same chapter in several of my other books to introduce the reader to essential elements of this field. Once you've read this chapter, you'll be prepared to read the rest of the material since the foundational essence of the components of autonomous AI driverless self-driving cars will have been established for you.

———————

When I give presentations about self-driving cars and teach classes on the topic, I have found it helpful to provide a framework around which the various key elements of self-driving cars can be understood and organized (see diagram at the end of this chapter). The framework needs to be simple enough to convey the overarching elements, but at the same time not so simple that it belies the true complexity of self-driving cars. As such, I am going to describe the framework here and try to offer in a thousand words (or more!) what the framework diagram itself intends to portray.

The core elements on the diagram are numbered for ease of reference. The numbering does not suggest any kind of prioritization of the elements. Each element is crucial. Each element has a purpose, and otherwise would not be included in the framework. For some self-driving cars, a particular element might be more important or somehow distinguished in comparison to other self-driving cars.

You could even use the framework to rate a particular self-driving car, doing so by gauging how well it performs in each of the elements of the framework. I will describe each of the elements, one at a time. After doing so, I'll discuss aspects that illustrate how the elements interact and perform during the overall effort of a self-driving car.

At the Cybernetic Self-Driving Car Institute, we use the framework to keep track of what we are working on, and how we are developing software that fills in what is needed to achieve Level 5 self-driving cars.

D-01: Sensor Capture

Let's start with the one element that often gets the most attention in the press about self-driving cars, namely, the sensory devices for a self-driving car.

On the framework, the box labeled as D-01 indicates "Sensor Capture" and refers to the processes of the self-driving car that involve collecting data from the myriad of sensors that are used for a self-driving car. The types of devices typically involved are listed, such as the use of mono cameras, stereo cameras, LIDAR devices, radar systems, ultrasonic devices, GPS, IMU, and so on.

These devices are tasked with obtaining data about the status of the self-driving car and the world around it. Some of the devices are continually providing updates, while others of the devices await an indication by the self-driving car that the device is supposed to collect data. The data might be first transformed in some fashion by the device itself, or it might instead be fed directly into the sensor capture as raw data. At that point, it might be up to the sensor capture processes to do transformations on the data. This all varies depending upon the nature of the devices being used and how the devices were designed and developed.

D-02: Sensor Fusion

Imagine that your eyeballs receive visual images, your nose receives odors, your ears receive sounds, and in essence each of your distinct sensory devices is getting some form of input. The input befits the nature of the device. Likewise, for a self-driving car, the cameras provide visual images, the radar returns radar reflections, and so on.

Each device provides the data as befits what the device does.

At some point, using the analogy to humans, you need to merge together what your eyes see, what your nose smells, what your ears hear, and piece it all together into a larger sense of what the world is all about and what is happening around you. Sensor fusion is the action of taking the singular aspects from each of the devices and putting them together into a larger puzzle.

Sensor fusion is a tough task. There are some devices that might not be working at the time of the sensor capture. Or, there might some devices that are unable to report well what they have detected. Again, using a human analogy, suppose you are in a dark room and so your eyes cannot see much. At that point, you might need to rely more so on your ears and what you hear. The same is true for a self-driving car. If the cameras are obscured due to snow and sleet, it might be that the radar can provide a greater indication of what the external conditions consist of.

In the case of a self-driving car, there can be a plethora of such sensory devices. Each is reporting what it can. Each might have its difficulties. Each might have its limitations, such as how far ahead it can detect an object. All of these limitations need to be considered during the sensor fusion task.

D-03: Virtual World Model

For humans, we presumably keep in our minds a model of the world around us when we are driving a car. In your mind, you know that the car is going at say 60 miles per hour and that you are on a freeway. You have a model in your mind that your car is surrounded by other cars, and that there are lanes to the freeway. Your model is not only based on what you can see, hear, etc., but also what you know about the nature of the world. You know that at any moment that car ahead of you can smash on its brakes, or the car behind you can ram into your car, or that the truck in the next lane might swerve into your lane.

The AI of the self-driving car needs to have a virtual world model, which it then keeps updated with whatever it is receiving from the sensor fusion, which received its input from the sensor capture and the sensory devices.

D-04: System Action Plan

By having a virtual world model, the AI of the self-driving car is able to keep track of where the car is and what is happening around the car. In addition, the AI needs to determine what to do next. Should the self-driving car hit its brakes? Should the self-driving car stay in its lane or swerve into the lane to the left? Should the self-driving car accelerate or slow down?

A system action plan needs to be prepared by the AI of the self-driving car. The action plan specifies what actions should be taken. The actions need to pertain to the status of the virtual world model. Plus, the actions need to be realizable.

This realizability means that the AI cannot just assert that the self-driving car should suddenly sprout wings and fly. Instead, the AI must be bound by whatever the self-driving car can actually do, such as coming to a halt in a distance of X feet at a speed of Y miles per hour, rather than perhaps asserting that the self-driving car come to a halt in 0 feet as though it could instantaneously come to a stop while it is in motion.

D-05: Controls Activation

The system action plan is implemented by activating the controls of the car to act according to what the plan stipulates. This might mean that the accelerator control is commanded to increase the speed of the car. Or, the steering control is commanded to turn the steering wheel 30 degrees to the left or right.

One question arises as to whether or not the controls respond as they are commanded to do. In other words, suppose the AI has commanded the accelerator to increase, but for some reason it does not do so. Or, maybe it tries to do so, but the speed of the car does not increase. The controls activation feeds back into the virtual world model, and simultaneously the virtual world model is getting updated from the sensors, the sensor capture, and the sensor fusion. This allows the AI to ascertain what has taken place as a result of the controls being commanded to take some kind of action.

By the way, please keep in mind that though the diagram seems to have a linear progression to it, the reality is that these are all aspects of the self-driving car that are happening in parallel and simultaneously. The sensors are capturing data, meanwhile the sensor fusion is taking place, meanwhile the virtual model is being updated, meanwhile the system action plan is being formulated and reformulated, meanwhile the controls are being activated.

This is the same as a human being that is driving a car. They are eyeballing the road, meanwhile they are fusing in their mind the sights, sounds, etc., meanwhile their mind is updating their model of the world around them, meanwhile they are formulating an action plan of what to do, and meanwhile they are pushing their foot onto the pedals and steering the car. In the normal course of driving a car, you are doing all of these at once. I mention this so that when you look at the diagram, you will think of the boxes as processes that are all happening at the same time, and not as though only one happens and then the next.

They are shown diagrammatically in a simplistic manner to help comprehend what is taking place. You though should also realize that they are working in parallel and simultaneous with each other. This is a tough aspect in that the inter-element communications involve latency and other aspects that must be taken into account. There can be delays in one element updating and then sharing its latest status with other elements.

D-06: Automobile & CAN

Contemporary cars use various automotive electronics and a Controller Area Network (CAN) to serve as the components that underlie the driving aspects of a car. There are Electronic Control Units (ECU's) which control subsystems of the car, such as the engine, the brakes, the doors, the windows, and so on.

The elements D-01, D-02, D-03, D-04, D-05 are layered on top of the D-06, and must be aware of the nature of what the D-06 is able to do and not do.

D-07: In-Car Commands

Humans are going to be occupants in self-driving cars. In a Level 5 self-driving car, there must be some form of communication that takes place between the humans and the self-driving car. For example, I go into a self-driving car and tell it that I want to be driven over to Disneyland, and along the way I want to stop at In-and-Out Burger. The self-driving car now parses what I've said and tries to then establish a means to carry out my wishes.

In-car commands can happen at any time during a driving journey. Though my example was about an in-car command when I first got into my self-driving car, it could be that while the self-driving car is carrying out the journey that I change my mind. Perhaps after getting stuck in traffic, I tell the self-driving car to forget about getting the burgers and just head straight over to the theme park. The self-driving car needs to be alert to in-car commands throughout the journey.

D-08: V2X Communications

We will ultimately have self-driving cars communicating with each other, doing so via V2V (Vehicle-to-Vehicle) communications. We will also have self-driving cars that communicate with the roadways and other aspects of the transportation infrastructure, doing so via V2I (Vehicle-to-Infrastructure).

The variety of ways in which a self-driving car will be communicating with other cars and infrastructure is being called V2X, whereby the letter X means whatever else we identify as something that a car should or would want to communicate with. The V2X communications will be taking place simultaneous with everything else on the diagram, and those other elements will need to incorporate whatever it gleans from those V2X communications.

D-09: Deep Learning

The use of Deep Learning permeates all other aspects of the self-driving car. The AI of the self-driving car will be using deep learning to do a better job at the systems action plan, and at the controls activation, and at the sensor fusion, and so on.

Currently, the use of artificial neural networks is the most prevalent form of deep learning. Based on large swaths of data, the neural networks attempt to "learn" from the data and therefore direct the efforts of the self-driving car accordingly.

D-10: Tactical AI

Tactical AI is the element of dealing with the moment-to-moment driving of the self-driving car. Is the self-driving car staying in its lane of the freeway? Is the car responding appropriately to the controls commands? Are the sensory devices working?

For human drivers, the tactical equivalent can be seen when you watch a novice driver such as a teenager that is first driving. They are focused on the mechanics of the driving task, keeping their eye on the road while also trying to properly control the car.

D-11: Strategic AI

The Strategic AI aspects of a self-driving car are dealing with the larger picture of what the self-driving car is trying to do. If I had asked that the self-driving car take me to Disneyland, there is an overall journey map that needs to be kept and maintained.

There is an interaction between the Strategic AI and the Tactical AI. The Strategic AI is wanting to keep on the mission of the driving, while the Tactical AI is focused on the particulars underway in the driving effort. If the Tactical AI seems to wander away from the overarching mission, the Strategic AI wants to see why and get things back on track. If the Tactical AI realizes that there is something amiss on the self-driving car, it needs to alert the Strategic AI accordingly and have an adjustment to the overarching mission that is underway.

D-12: Self-Aware AI

Very few of the self-driving cars being developed are including a Self-Aware AI element, which we at the Cybernetic Self-Driving Car Institute believe is crucial to Level 5 self-driving cars.

The Self-Aware AI element is intended to watch over itself, in the sense that the AI is making sure that the AI is working as intended. Suppose you had a human driving a car, and they were starting to drive erratically. Hopefully, their own self-awareness would make them realize they themselves are driving poorly, such as perhaps starting to fall asleep after having been driving for hours on end. If you had a passenger in the car, they might be able to alert the driver if the driver is starting to do something amiss. This is exactly what the Self-Aware

AI element tries to do, it becomes the overseer of the AI, and tries to detect when the AI has become faulty or confused, and then find ways to overcome the issue.

D-13: Economic

The economic aspects of a self-driving car are not per se a technology aspect of a self-driving car, but the economics do indeed impact the nature of a self-driving car. For example, the cost of outfitting a self-driving car with every kind of possible sensory device is prohibitive, and so choices need to be made about which devices are used. And, for those sensory devices chosen, whether they would have a full set of features or a more limited set of features.

We are going to have self-driving cars that are at the low-end of a consumer cost point, and others at the high-end of a consumer cost point. You cannot expect that the self-driving car at the low-end is going to be as robust as the one at the high-end. I realize that many of the self-driving car pundits are acting as though all self-driving cars will be the same, but they won't be. Just like anything else, we are going to have self-driving cars that have a range of capabilities. Some will be better than others. Some will be safer than others. This is the way of the real-world, and so we need to be thinking about the economics aspects when considering the nature of self-driving cars.

D-14: Societal

This component encompasses the societal aspects of AI which also impacts the technology of self-driving cars. For example, the famous Trolley Problem involves what choices should a self-driving car make when faced with life-and-death matters. If the self-driving car is about to either hit a child standing in the roadway, or instead ram into a tree at the side of the road and possibly kill the humans in the self-driving car, which choice should be made?

We need to keep in mind the societal aspects will underlie the AI of the self-driving car. Whether we are aware of it explicitly or not, the AI will have embedded into it various societal assumptions.

D-15: Innovation

I included the notion of innovation into the framework because we can anticipate that whatever a self-driving car consists of, it will continue to be innovated over time. The self-driving cars coming out in the next several years will undoubtedly be different and less innovative than the versions that come out in ten years hence, and so on.

Framework Overall

For those of you that want to learn about self-driving cars, you can potentially pick a particular element and become specialized in that aspect. Some engineers are focusing on the sensory devices. Some engineers focus on the controls activation. And so on. There are specialties in each of the elements.

Researchers are likewise specializing in various aspects. For example, there are researchers that are using Deep Learning to see how best it can be used for sensor fusion. There are other researchers that are using Deep Learning to derive good System Action Plans. Some are studying how to develop AI for the Strategic aspects of the driving task, while others are focused on the Tactical aspects.

A well-prepared all-around software developer that is involved in self-driving cars should be familiar with all of the elements, at least to the degree that they know what each element does. This is important since whatever piece of the pie that the software developer works on, they need to be knowledgeable about what the other elements are doing.

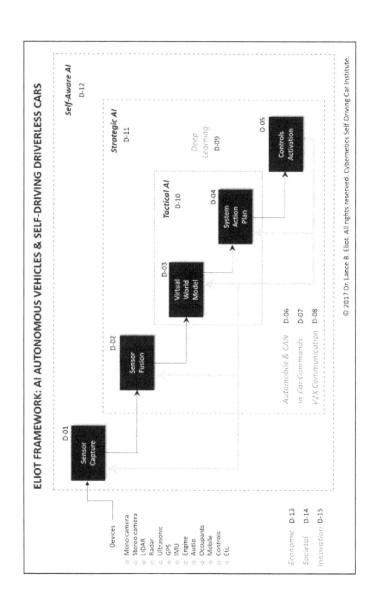

Lance B. Eliot

CHAPTER 2
YOUR BUCKET LIST
AND
AI SELF-DRIVING CARS

CHAPTER 2

YOUR BUCKET LIST
AND AI SELF-DRIVING CARS

Have you put together your bucket list?

If you don't know what a bucket list is, you must be living inside a deep cave that lacks internet access.

A bucket list is simply a list of the things you'd like to do before you pass from this earth.

Origins of the phrase seem to emanate from the old saying that when you die you will kick the bucket.

As the story goes, the writer of the 2007 movie entitled "The Bucket List" had created his own list of the activities and places he'd like to go to before he should die, and after mulling over the list, he conceived of the clever moniker *bucket list* and then used the catchy phrase for the title of the film.

An entire cottage industry seems to have sprung forth that offers to help you craft your bucket list, along with aiding in fulfilling your bucket list.

Though some of those providing such aid might be doing so out of the goodness of their hearts, the bottom line is that money is to be made from people's bucket lists.

If you are a travel agent, for those still around, it is wondrous to have a shopping list of the places that someone wants to go, making it much easier to book those cruise ships and flights and get your piece of the action.

Tourist destinations love the bucket lists. Hotels love the bucket lists. Essentially, any element of the travel industry is all in favor of bucket lists.

Just in case that seems overly cynical, let's go ahead and agree that indeed having a bucket list is good for people, giving them a structured way to ponder their future.

For some people, a bucket list is a type of wish list that gives them the energy and life-force needed to continue in their existing day-to-day grueling efforts. For each time that your boss yells at you, or that you get into a fender bender, you still have in the back of your mind that vaunted bucket list.

Someday, when the time comes, you'll be in a much better mood and place, since you'll gradually try to accomplish all the visits and activities you've laid out in the list.

Without having a bucket list, you might not have anything tangible to keep your daily spirits up. Furthermore, you might reach retirement and feel an overbearing sense of emptiness of what to do next, when instead your retirement presumably frees up your time to tackle the bucket list items that have gradually accumulated over the years.

It is interesting to see how much agony and quite debatable advice seems to now underlie bucket lists.

One example of conflicting advice is based on the sage wisdom (by some) that you should never remove an item from your bucket list once you've written it down. Their argument is that if you put a task onto the list, you should "own it" and have the nerve to fulfill the item. It is a sign of weakness and cowardness to remove an item from the list, they say.

Others that offer contrary advice will tell you that over time your interests and tastes are bound to change. Items that you put onto your bucket list when you were in your 40's might not seem as important anymore when you are in your 60's. It is fine to change the bucket list as you grow older, becoming wiser about what are the important things to do in your life.

Another somewhat confusing bit of advice involves *when* you should partake in the bucket list tasks.

Get to the bucket list items right away, before you get weary and your bones are creaking, some will tell you. Others point out that by waiting to undertake the bucket list items, you can savor their eventual frolic and fun that will result. No sense in hurriedly doing items that are supposed to be done as you get older and can really appreciate them more fully.

There's another kind of twist involved about the bucket list items.

Should the bucket list consist solely of the most extraordinary and outlandish places or tasks that you can conceive of?

Maybe your bucket list should have you going sky diving, along with climbing each of the topmost mountain peaks and going to see the pyramids and other praised wonders of the world.

Not everyone believes though that the bucket list must be the impossible dream kind of stuff.

You might have seemed small and mundane items on the list, but for which you've never had the time or attention to accomplish.

Learn to play the piano, volunteer to help out at a local school, become an amateur chef involving your favorite cuisine, these are all bucket list items that you could include, though they aren't as spectacular as the sky diving and other breathtaking and high-risk tasks that some say you are supposed to want to do before you die.

Here's an item I'd suggest you include on your bucket list: *Make use of a true self-driving car.*

Before I further elaborate, do you think that the bucket list item about self-driving cars should be in the same clump as the high-risk high adventure set or is it more rightfully placed into the camp of achieving on everyday activities?

Let's unpack the matter and see.

The Levels Of Self-Driving Cars

It is important to clarify what I mean when referring to true self-driving cars.

True self-driving cars are ones that the AI drives the car entirely on its own and there isn't any human assistance during the driving task.

These driverless cars are considered a Level 4 and Level 5, while a car that requires a human driver to co-share the driving effort is usually considered at a Level 2 or Level 3. The cars that co-share the driving task are described as being semi-autonomous, and typically contain a variety of automated add-ons that are referred to as ADAS (Advanced Driver-Assistance Systems).

There is not yet a true self-driving car at Level 5, which we don't yet even know if this will be possible to achieve, and nor how long it will take to get there.

Meanwhile, the Level 4 efforts are gradually trying to get some traction by undergoing very narrow and selective public roadway trials, though there is controversy over whether this testing should be allowed per se (we are all life-or-death guinea pigs in an experiment taking place on our highways and byways, some point out).

Since the semi-autonomous cars require a human driver, such cars aren't particularly significant to the bucket list matter.

There is essentially no difference between using a Level 2 or Level 3 versus a conventional car when it comes to driving and therefore doesn't merit a spot on the bucket list.

It is notable to point out that in spite of those idiots that keep posting videos of themselves falling asleep at the wheel of a Level 2 or Level 3 car, do not be misled into believing that you can take away your attention from the driving task while driving a semi-autonomous car.

You are the responsible party for the driving actions of the car, regardless of how much automation might be tossed into a Level 2 or Level 3.

Worthiness For Bucket List Inclusion

Let's focus on the inclusion of *true* self-driving cars onto your bucket list, meaning driverless cars that are in the Level 4 and Level 5 categories.

One aspect of any item on a bucket list is the feasibility of accomplishing the item.

If you put onto your bucket list that you want to visit the planet Jupiter, I don't think you have much chance of getting there within your lifetime.

In terms of self-driving cars, you have a very good chance of riding in a Level 4 driverless car.

Score that as a win for your bucket list.

In fact, if you live in some areas such as Phoenix, Las Vegas, Silicon Valley, Pittsburgh, etc., you can likely arrange for a Level 4 ride, though it takes some wrangling to do so.

There are people today riding in Level 4's, somewhat so, and thus this is not an outwardly wild item for the list. People that are riding in them would even say it is rather mundane.

Of course, there are lots of skydivers that exist today, and they would likewise say that putting sky diving onto your list is "mundane" in their eyes.

There are though some tricks involved in this.

For example, by-and-large all of the Level 4 efforts include a back-up "safety" operator in the car, ready to take over the driving from the AI system if needed.

Strictly speaking, one could argue that going in a Level 4 that has a back-up driver is not the spirit of being inside a true Level 4 car. Purists would say that only if you have a fully safe and comfortable ride in a Level 4 that has no back-up human driver would it count as a serious and sincere kind of Level 4 ride.

Some liken these fine details as equivalent to whether going sky diving counts if you are strapped to another parachutist. Is that true sky diving?

Self-driving car purists would eschew that analogy and say that today's Level 4's is more like going sky diving in a wind tunnel.

Anyway, we can go back-and-forth about the Level 4 aspects, including another notable facet that Level 4's of today tend to exist in very constrained ODD's (Operational Design Domains).

Yes, the proper definition of Level 4 allows for stipulating the scope of where a driverless car might be able to go on its own, but some say that the existing ODD's are overly narrow and limited.

Overall, the odds are that we'll gradually be witnessing a rollout of the Level 4's over the next several years, and your chances of riding in one will increasingly rise (assuming that no calamities occur that cause a slowing down or stoppage toward achieving true self-driving cars).

Level 4 is a relatively achievable inclusion onto your bucket list.

I suppose you might be asking why you should care about putting the Level 4 ride as worthy of the things you'll do before you die.

You've got to admit that the notion of having an AI system, a kind of robot, being able to drive a car, doing so without a human driver, well, it's a dream come true for anyone that has watched a science fiction movie or read sci-fi books.

And though the car still looks like a car, the amount of computer power and AI capabilities required to drive a car in the same manner as humans is an incredible feat of engineering and computer science.

Plus, though it might seem like outstretched hyperbole, achieving true self-driving cars is something that one could consider being added to the top wonders of mankind. That being said, once self-driving cars become a routine part of our existence, we'll look at them as commonplace, like the advent of mobile phones, and perhaps forget how hard it was to achieve such an amazing accomplishment.

Next, consider whether your bucket list ought to mention Level 5.

That's an entirely different animal, one might say.

Generally, a Level 5 self-driving car is supposed to be able to drive, without a human driver, in any circumstance for which a human driver could drive a car.

In contrast, a Level 4 being fielded by an automaker or tech firm might be defined as not being able to drive on its own whenever the weather has turned foul, such as if it is snowing. Humans can often drive while it is snowing, though it might be dicey, and at some point, the snow might become excessive and prevent further driving.

In any case, it could be that a Level 4 is not able to deal with the visual obstructions and radar-like clutter that snow provides and therefore the ODD might say that this specific Level 4 won't drive in the snow. If snow begins to appear while Level 4 is already underway, it would likely pull over to the side of the road and wait for the snow to cease.

A human driver is bound to try and drive in snowy weather. Whatever a human driver might be able to pull off, in theory, a Level 5 should be able to do the same.

As mentioned earlier, there isn't any Level 5 today and we don't know how or when we will see a true Level 5.

It's a pretty steep hill of cognitive-like savviness to be able to get an AI system to drive a car in the manner that a human driver would at any time and any place be able to drive a car.

Probably best to have millennials put the Level 5 onto their bucket list, rather than those beyond that age bracket.

We might get Level 5 sooner, maybe, and at least we can hope that's the case.

Conclusion

Sometimes an item on a bucket list will have an added component that makes it especially difficult or challenging to perform the item.

A skydiver wouldn't put plain vanilla sky diving on their bucket list since they presumably are already actively doing sky diving.

They might put onto their list to do a skydive from an extremely high altitude, perhaps aiming to do what Felix Baumgartner did in October 2012 when he leaped from a height of 128,000 feet above earth (the famous "stunt" sponsored by Red Bull).

For those of you that are toying with putting the act of riding in a self-driving car as an item onto your bucket list, you might consider juicing it up.

Here's an idea for you.

Pledge to take a ride in a true self-driving car that will allow you to journey across the entire United States, undertaking the now-classic family vacation trip to see our great country, but doing so via a self-driving car that does all the driving for you.

Essentially, this would most likely have to be a Level 5, unless somehow there was a Level 4 that had enough overlapping ODD's that it could make its way across the country, and assuming that no tricks were being used (such as a remote human operator, or doing this only when the weather lined-up perfectly, etc.).

Whatever you decide to put onto your own bucket list, I hope you enjoy the things that you opt to do before you expire.

Self-driving cars might be a ho-hum for you, and maybe you are holding out for the autonomous flying cars instead.

Good luck!

CHAPTER 3
HIGHWAY STUNTS
AND
AI SELF-DRIVING TRUCKS

CHAPTER 3

HIGHWAY STUNTS
AND
AI SELF-DRIVING TRUCKS

I like a feel-good story as much as the next person.

There has been a recent spate of media gushing about self-driving semi-trailer trucks, heralding the vaunted arrival of driverless big trucks due to one or another automaker or tech firm having made a publicity related stunt involving a highway journey debut, including usually carrying along a noteworthy load of produce or products from point A to point B.

This kind of feat oftentimes gets pundits into a lather of speculating that self-driving capabilities for large-scale trucks are nearly ready for primetime and implying that the self-driving tech involved is akin to a Level 5 fully Autonomous Vehicle (more on this in a moment).

The most recent news-making trek occurred last week.

Reportedly, a semi-trailer truck hauling about 40,000 pounds of butter went on a three-day journey across the United States, starting in Tulare, California and ending in Quakertown, Pennsylvania, and did so (apparently) predominantly in driverless mode as equipped by Plus.ai, an up-and-coming self-driving vehicle startup company based in Silicon Valley.

The delivery was a real one in that Land O'Lakes had wanted the butter hauled from California to Pennsylvania and so the journey accomplished two birds in one stone, namely delivering the needed butter and showcasing driverless capabilities for trucking and giving Plus.ai some media attention.

According to news accounts, there was both a safety back-up driver and a system engineer in the truck throughout the trip.

The safety back-up driver would have likely been in a position to rapidly take over the truck if a disengagement was needed (note that "disengagement" is industry parlance for when a human back-up driver takes over the wheel from the AI system that's driving). The ride-along system engineer likely monitored the internal status of the on-board computers and AI, regularly scanning the sensory input being collected and monitoring the AI's status during the trip.

Allegedly, the journey took place without any disengagements.

The reason that the trek took three days, which is longer than the time it would take to straight-out have the AI drive non-stop across the U.S. (no need for the AI to rest or get coffee), apparently was to give the human back-up driver the federally mandated breaks required when doing truck hauling.

Reporters touted this butter delivering journey as an incredible feat that demonstrates the advent of true self-driving trucks.

Many commentators also held this accomplishment over the heads of the self-driving car makers, trying to make the driverless car builders appear to be behind-the-times and dis them as dismal laggards in comparison to driverless big haul makers.

As I said, I like a feel-good story, but it would also be helpful if the media didn't rush to judgment, including having the press render outlandish comments or unsupported declarations that are fanciful and not in keeping with the facts.

Let's unpack the matter and unravel the truth.

The Levels Of Self-Driving Vehicles

It is important to clarify what I mean when referring to true self-driving vehicles.

True self-driving vehicles are ones that the AI drives the car or truck entirely on its own and there isn't any human assistance during the driving task.

These driverless vehicles are considered a Level 4 and Level 5, while a car or truck that requires a human driver to co-share the driving effort is usually considered at a Level 2 or Level 3. The vehicles that co-share the driving task are described as being semi-autonomous, and typically contain a variety of automated add-ons that are referred to as ADAS (Advanced Driver-Assistance Systems).

There is not yet a true self-driving vehicle at Level 5, which we don't yet even know if this will be possible to achieve, and nor how long it will take to get there.

Meanwhile, the Level 4 efforts are gradually trying to get some traction by undergoing very narrow and selective public roadway trials, though there is controversy over whether this testing should be allowed per se (we are all life-or-death guinea pigs in an experiment taking place on our highways and byways, some point out).

Since semi-autonomous vehicles require a human driver, the adoption of those types of cars or trucks won't be markedly different than driving conventional vehicles, so I'm not going to include them in this discussion about self-driving big hauls.

For semi-autonomous vehicles, it is equally important that I mention a disturbing aspect that's been arising, namely that in spite of those human drivers that keep posting videos of themselves falling asleep at the wheel of a Level 2 or Level 3 car, we all need to avoid being misled into believing that the driver can take away their attention from the driving task while driving a semi-autonomous car or truck.

You are the responsible party for the driving actions of the vehicle, regardless of how much automation might be tossed into a Level 2 or Level 3.

Self-Driving Vehicles And The Truth

For Level 4 and Level 5 true self-driving vehicles, there won't be a human driver involved in the driving task.

All occupants will be passengers.

A self-driving vehicle at a Level 4 is less capable than being at a Level 5.

Generally, Level 4 is a self-imposed scope delineation in terms of where and when the self-driving capability will function, referred to as the Operational Design Domain (ODD) for the vehicle.

For example, I might make a self-driving AI system that can only cope with sunny weather conditions and works exclusively within a specific city boundary. That would be the ODD for any vehicle using my self-driving tech. If it is raining, the AI would refuse to drive the vehicle, and likewise, if you wanted to go outside the city bounds the AI would indicate it was unable to do so.

Level 5 is essentially a no-ODD constrained form of self-driving tech. A true Level 5 would be able to drive anywhere that a human could drive a vehicle, including in any kind of weather or place that a human was able to do the driving.

In the case of the butter delivery story, the Plus.ai company acknowledges that they are currently working on and testing at a Level 4, not a Level 5 capability.

I mention this facet since the mass media doesn't oftentimes understand and nor convey the difference between being at a Level 4 versus at a Level 5 (it's a huge difference!).

Now, don't misunderstand my point as though I am somehow knocking the efforts of achieving a Level 4. I'm decidedly not knocking it.

Just about everyone in the self-driving realm is aiming right now at Level 4, including the self-driving car makers and the self-driving truck makers, doing so as the cornerstone step toward ultimately reaching the vaunted Level 5.

Accomplishing Level 4 is a tremendous step in of itself, so don't falsely denigrate it as somehow just a minor stepping stone.

Getting to true Level 4 for any kind of expansive ODD is a wonderful accomplishment and will have substantive benefits for providing self-driving capabilities to society.

My carping about this butter story is that the media implied or at times stated that true self-driving has arrived, which is false on several accounts:

- First, this was only a tryout run and it is mistaken to extrapolate the experiment into saying that self-driving has been solved.

- Second, this and other such tryouts are about Level 4, and not a showing of Level 5, thus the experiment is about ODD-constrained self-driving and not about the elusive full self-driving.

Why are such nuances important?

The media is fanning confusion among the public and regulators, doing so by declaring prematurely that full and complete self-driving has been achieved, and the next day trouncing self-driving and offering the opinion that it won't ever occur.

These kinds of good cop and bad cop spasms of storytelling about self-driving aren't helping anyone other than the press that wants to get heightened ratings for their news reports.

I'd also like to tackle the comparisons being made or implied about cars versus trucks in the self-driving realm.

Does a seemingly self-driving truck that goes on a cross-country trek mean that somehow the big haul self-driving is lightyears ahead of the self-driving car tech?

No.

There is nothing magically better or supreme for self-driving truck tech than there is for self-driving car tech.

It's all pretty much the same.

The key difference between self-driving for trucks versus cars is more so about the nature of trucks and what they do, rather than the self-driving tech itself.

I'll explore that next.

Self-Driving Trucks And What They Do

Semi-trailer hauling trucks are big and heavy vehicles, while cars are generally much lighter and smaller in size.

I think we can all agree to that proviso.

Highway driving is usually markedly different than say downtown street driving, notably due to the fact that highway driving involves primarily straight-ahead driving with an occasional lane change, and thus there aren't as many turns or complex driving as would be found in a downtown area.

Furthermore, highways are usually devoid of pedestrians, bicyclists, and others that might get in the way of driving.

I'm not saying there is never such obstructions on highways and just pointing out that street-level driving typically involves an ongoing, persistent, and intensified cacophony of disruptions and potential object collisions that need to be continually coped with.

I hope we can all agree with that stipulation.

As such, when you test self-driving tech on a vehicle that's on the highway, you aren't necessarily simultaneously testing as though that tech can also handle driving on side streets and downtown areas.

In some respects, a car or truck that you put onto a highway can almost be like a train, staying within its lane for long periods of time, and making various lane changes only as needed. Trains have the luxury of being on a railroad track and so don't need to do much in terms of being able to drive, at least not in the sense of human driving per se.

Whenever you hear about a self-driving vehicle that was tested on a highway, you must ask whether that tryout included only highway driving or also includes off-highway driving too.

Recall the infamous Uber Otto self-driving semi-hauler truck that made a 120-mile run to deliver beer (see my debunking of what happened).

For some of these self-driving truck tryouts, the human back-up driver is utilized to get the truck to the highway, and once the highway driving is begun the AI is switched on. Then, after going whatever distance or time might be involved, the human back-up driver turns-off the AI and drives the truck off the highway to a rest stop or to the targeted delivery warehouse.

Therefore, when headlines blare that a self-driving truck delivered milk or pajamas, we don't really know whether the self-driving was employed only while on the highway or also on the side streets leading to and from the highway.

Plus, even if the side streets were used, another handy trick is to have pre-mapped just the stretch between the starting point and the highway entrance, so that the AI is prepared for that first part of the trek. And, you can aim to do that portion in the early morning hours, before much traffic has developed on the side streets.

All in all, as might be evident, there are plenty of ways to make the trek much easier for the AI and yet the media fails to ask questions and probe as to the details of the journey that was performed.

A banner headline that says a big haul truck delivered a load of peanuts is raft with assumptions such as the AI of the truck was able to deal with the difficulties of getting onto the highways and off the highways, when needed, as needed, along with having driven on the highways themselves.

We don't know that to be the case.

Another facet of big truck driving is that usually a human truck driver tries to minimize the number of lane changes and stays in the slow lane of traffic (often as mandated by regulations).

Again, this is unlike car driving in that a human car driver often gets into and out of lanes on a frequent basis. They opt to dart over to the fast lane, then change lanes to get around a car here or there and are navigating in and around the rest of the traffic.

There is a lot of discretion in driving.

I remember that my grandparents would get onto the freeway and stay entirely in the slow lane. They never ventured out of it. They clung to the right side of the freeway with dear life. During their time on the freeways, they were counting the miles and minutes to reach the off-ramp they would be taking.

I think we can all agree that driving in such a limited fashion is different in tone and complexity than when freewheeling amongst the beehive of freeway traffic.

Yet another facet about semi-trailer trucks is that they are big and imposing.

Much of the time, cars keep away from the big trucks.

Wherever the truck wants to go, cars get out of the way. It's like a big dog that causes the little puppies to scatter.

This can make things easier for the AI.

The AI might be driving a big haul truck with not much finesse and relying upon the bulk and fierceness of the imposing truck to spark the rest of traffic to get out of its way.

I realize that any experienced truck driver will have angst about this characterization of highway driving and point out that car drivers do lots of stupid things, such as cutting in front of a big haul or riding on the bumper of a big haul.

Yes, those are absolutely valid aspects that involve true truck driving.

But we don't know that any particular tryout of a self-driving big truck on a highway involved those kinds of occasions.

Maybe so, maybe not.

In fact, believe it or not, there have been self-driving truck highway stunts whereby those undertaking the effort had brought human-driven cars onto the highway that road next to the truck, serving as guardians while the truck made its trek. Those defensive position cars would attempt to keep other traffic from getting in the way of the truck.

Smart?

Sneaky?

You decide.

Nobody readily knew about these hidden angel efforts and so the media went along with assuming that the truck has entirely done the trek on its own, yet the reality was that a plethora of guide vehicles driven by humans surrounded the truck during its journey in a kind of safety cocoon.

Conclusion

There are several ways that the media could do a better job of reporting on self-driving truck efforts.

One aspect would be to find out the underlying details of a stunt or trek that is being reported on.

Besides an indication of how many disengagements there were, let's not stop with just that singular number since it can be somewhat meaningless depending upon how the driving task was structured and undertaken.

Questions abound such as:

- Did the trek involve the AI driving the entire journey, end-to-end, including when off the highway too?

- What was the complexity of the traffic and driving while off the highway?

- While on the highway, how much of the time did the truck stay in its lane and do straight-ahead driving?

- How many lane changes occurred?

- What was the complexity of the lane changes?

- How many times did nearby car traffic attempt an incursion into the truck driving and in what ways did the AI deal with those incursions (did it overly rely on its bullying factor to prevail over the cars)?

- What was the number of encounters with other trucks and navigating around say slower moving trucks or otherwise contending with fellow trucks nearby (presumably human-driven trucks)?

- Did the truck encounter highway debris or other unexpected and unplanned difficulties, and if so, how did the AI respond?

- Did the AI system abide overtly by the state-by-state driving regulations as it went cross-country?

- Were there any close calls and if so, how did the AI driving system react?

- Was the truck alone or did it have added help from allied support vehicles during the trek?

- Etc.

Some suggest that these trucking tryout efforts ought to have an unbiased third-party "auditor" that goes along during the trip, being able to witness first-hand what happens, doing so to augment whatever claims are later made about the journey.

By the way, the third-party shouldn't be someone that can have the wool pooled over their eyes, which oftentimes is done by asking a junior reporter that doesn't know squat about self-driving tech to go along.

Finally, there are critics that argue these big truck tryouts on our highways are the worst kind of guinea pig experiments of self-driving tech.

Allow me to elaborate.

Having a human back-up driver during a self-driving vehicle tryout is not a guarantee that a crash is not going to occur. Take a look at the sad and now famous incident of the Uber self-driving car in Arizona that rammed and killed a pedestrian at nighttime that was jaywalking, and you'll see that the human back-up driver was apparently not paying attention to the driving task at the time of the incident.

It's one thing to have a car go awry and cause an accident while having a large semi-trailer truck do so could be even worse.

The human back-up driver in the truck might be caught unawares after hours upon hours of not driving and be lulled into believing that the AI is doing just fine. They might be delayed in responding to a rapidly emerging dilemma.

Some question whether the self-driving truck (and self-driving car) efforts are prematurely using our pubic roadways, and ought to be focusing instead on more testing at proving grounds or via simulations, waiting until better prepared to use our open highways and byways.

Anyway, the odds are that we are going to continue to have highway tryouts of both self-driving trucks and self-driving cars.

The self-driving truck stories are eye-catching since we all tend to think of driving a truck as a rough and tough chore and if a truck can do self-driving its awesome to imagine, perhaps more so than driving an everyday and mundane car.

Of course, human truck drivers aren't as enamored of the looming day of AI driving trucks, but it's a day that will eventually arrive, presumably reducing the costs of hauling goods and making our roads safer, assuming that the AI is appropriately readied and capable to do the driving.

Self-driving tech firms and automakers that carryout public tryouts of big haul trucks can help society understand the current state-of-the-art, limitations included, doing so by being upfront in a detailed manner about how they are undertaking their tryouts and how much more needs to be done.

The ads that urge people to go to truck driving school and earn a living via driving trucks will eventually give way as AI takes the wheel.

We decidedly aren't there yet.

CHAPTER 4

FUTURE WONDERMENT AND AI SELF-DRIVING CARS

CHAPTER 4

FUTURE WONDERMENT AND
AI SELF-DRIVING CARS

It's that wonderful time of the year!

The Christmas season is upon us and there is joy in the air.

Stores are festooned with ornaments and sparkling lights. Music is heard throughout the malls and you can't help but start to feel the spirit of giving and sharing. It is time to be joyous, spending time with family and friends, and relishing precious time of togetherness and good tidings.

Well, maybe it's not entirely so rosy and imbued with quaint mistletoe.

Frustrations admittedly abound.

Driving over to the store to get gifts can be an exasperating and beguiling chore.

You need to contend with horn-honking traffic jams.

Other drivers are frantic to get to their shopping destinations and oftentimes cut you off. Parking is a near impossibility. Fender benders are rampant as drivers squeeze into parking spots and emergency lanes that they shouldn't be using.

Reported cases of drivers getting out of their cars to punch each other over driving disputes catch headlines and road rage gets into gear.

Turns out that it is a dog-eat-dog world when it comes to getting your seasonal shopping undertaken.

Much of the time, you find yourself shaking your head in sadness and disgust that the holiday spirit seems to not enter people's minds when they are driving their cars, and instead they appear to be overcome by a selfish get-out-of-my-way take-no-prisoners attitude.

Even a quick trip to the local grocery store to stock up on holiday cookies or eggnog is rife with traffic and parking woes. A driving task that should take a few minutes gets extended into an hour of time, along with perhaps having someone wave their fist at you as they extoll that you've not been driving fast enough or be willing to speed through those yellow lights and roll through stop signs.

Of course, there's also the driving involved in getting to the house of your relatives for an extended family get together. More agony of being in snarled holiday traffic.

You might also be driving to holiday parties put on by work colleagues or attending holiday parties by associations that you are a member of.

Plus, many people opt to take vacation during this time of the year, dovetailing into company holiday granted time-off, and proceed to drive on long trips across their state or across the U.S.

According to national statistics, approximately 100 million Americans will travel 50 miles or more from home during the Christmas holiday period and nearly 90% of that travel is done on the roadways (versus flying or say taking a train).

Hopefully, all that maddening time spent on the busy roadways won't undermine your overall festive outlook, though it certainly can put a damper on your holiday excitement.

In short, there is way too much frustration and angst involved in the roadway traveling during the holidays and it's a darned shame that there's seemingly nothing that can be done to avert the anguish.

Wait a minute, maybe Santa has something for us that can help.

Here's a question to ponder: *Will the advent of true self-driving cars provide some relief from the holiday angst and aid in making the season as wonderful as it should be?*

I say yes.

Let's unpack the matter (and make sure to put a bow on it too).

The Levels Of Self-Driving Cars

It is important to clarify what I mean when referring to true self-driving cars.

True self-driving cars are ones that the AI drives the car entirely on its own and there isn't any human assistance during the driving task.

These driverless vehicles are considered a Level 4 and Level 5, while a car that requires a human driver to co-share the driving effort is usually considered at a Level 2 or Level 3. The cars that co-share the driving task are described as being semi-autonomous, and typically contain a variety of automated add-on's that are referred to as ADAS (Advanced Driver-Assistance Systems).

There is not yet a true self-driving car at Level 5, which we don't yet even know if this will be possible to achieve, and nor how long it will take to get there.

Meanwhile, the Level 4 efforts are gradually trying to get some traction by undergoing very narrow and selective public roadway trials, though there is controversy over whether this testing should be allowed per se (we are all life-or-death guinea pigs in an experiment taking place on our highways and byways, some point out).

Since semi-autonomous cars require a human driver, the adoption of those types of cars won't be markedly different than driving conventional vehicles, so I'm not going to include them in this discussion about the holidays.

For semi-autonomous cars, it is equally important that I mention a disturbing aspect that's been arising, namely that in spite of those human drivers that keep posting videos of themselves falling asleep at the wheel of a Level 2 or Level 3 car, we all need to avoid being misled into believing that the driver can take away their attention from the driving task while driving a semi-autonomous car.

You are the responsible party for the driving actions of the vehicle, regardless of how much automation might be tossed into a Level 2 or Level 3.

Self-Driving Cars And The Holidays

For Level 4 and Level 5 true self-driving vehicles, there won't be a human driver involved in the driving task.

All occupants will be passengers.

When you go to a mall, you won't be driving, and instead, the AI will do the driving for you.

Guess what?

This means that you no longer need to be the one that bears the frustration and angst of being at the wheel.

There you are, riding along in a true self-driving car, and letting your mind wander to dreams of sugarplums dancing and not needing to be aware that some idiot driver ahead of you is cutting off your car or going as slow as a snail.

Let the AI worry about it.

Furthermore, you can be watching videos or live streaming video while going over to the store, doing so by the likely addition of LED displays mounted inside the driverless car. The odds are that self-driving cars will have high-def displays and be connected to the Internet at top speeds such as 5G.

You can do a live connection with a loved one and via a Facetime-like interaction be able to discuss what gifts to get for friends and family.

Maybe have some eggnog during the drive, perhaps spiked (which you would never do as a driver), though please don't let things get out of hand (it would be unseemly to pour out of a driverless car and be as drunk as a skunk).

In terms of gift getting, we've already begun to see a large shift from going to brick-and-mortar stores to instead ordering online and having your packages delivered to your home. With true self-driving cars, most pundits predict that we'll increase dramatically the amount of home-delivered items since driverless cars will be able to drive those purchased packages to your house.

Family vacations will be easier to undertake too (see **my detailed explanation here**).

You and the family can enjoy the time together during a cross country road trip. Rather than the adults having to constantly trade-off doing the driving task, the AI will be doing the driving. This allows the adults to have fun with the kids while inside the driverless car, playing games and otherwise devoting attention that would have been going toward the driving chore.

Speaking of kids, another facet of driverless cars will be that children can get around to places without requiring an adult driver to be present and being there to drive the car.

Suppose you want the kids to get over to grandma's house and you aren't yet home to drive them. By using a self-driving car, the kids can pile into the vehicle and be driven by the AI, allowing you to get over to grandma's once your Scrooge boss lets you out of the office.

As an aside, there is some controversy about letting kids ride in driverless cars without having any adult supervision, and it is hard to imagine such a future, but there is a bona fide case to be made that we culturally might eventually change our views on this matter and find this to be a valid form of transport for non-adults.

Think about the other possibilities of how driverless cars can alleviate the stress and strain of the holidays.

A self-driving car can drop you at your destination and thus there's no need for you to deal with parking the car.

Toss out those crazy parking lot fisticuff moments since you won't ever need to be in a parking lot, to begin with, and toss out the annoying act of driving round and round to find a parking spot.

Some pundits are saying that we'll no longer have traffic congestion once we have self-driving cars, but that's a rather Utopian viewpoint. For many years to come, likely for decades, we are going to have a mixture of both conventional cars and self-driving cars on our roadways (there are about 250 million conventional cars today in the United States).

All in all, we are going to continue to have traffic congestion for a long time to come.

Yet, despite the traffic congestion, when you are inside a driverless car you might not especially notice that the traffic is backed-up. If you are watching a classic movie while inside a driverless car, such as *It's A Wonderful Life*, you probably won't care that a morass of cars is all backed-up and crawling along.

Another nifty aspect will be that people today that are mobility marginalized or disadvantaged will likely have greater mobility access due to the emergence of self-driving cars.

Maybe your elderly father is not able to drive a car and lives far away from the rest of the family. It might be logistically difficult for you to go pick him and up and drive him to a family holiday get together.

On the other hand, he could use a driverless car and show-up ready to enjoy some cherished time with you all.

That's truly a wonderful life moment.

More Reasons For Holiday Cheer

I'm not saying that driverless cars will erase or eradicate all the stress of the holidays.

No doubt, there will still be lots of holiday stress to be had.

At least you can have some contemplative meditation time while inside a driverless car.

Or, better still, use the time inside the self-driving car to catch some winks.

It is expected that most driverless cars will have reclining seats so that you can take a nap or go to sleep while on a driving journey. After a day's hard work, you can grab a nap on the way home, and feel refreshed when you walk in the door, greeting the rest of the family rather than snarling at them.

Something else is worth considering too about self-driving cars.

There are many that are hoping and expecting that driverless cars will save lives, meaning that the number of lives lost by car crashes and car injuries will be substantially reduced.

Currently, there are about 40,000 annual car-related deaths and approximately 2.7 million car-related injuries in the United States.

Take a somber moment to reflect on the fact that 40,000 people each year in the U.S. won't be celebrating the holidays with their loved ones due to being killed in a car crash.

And if that number doesn't seem disheartening enough, consider that over a decade or so of such loses amounts to 400,000 or more people killed in car crashes in America, or nearly a half million people consisting of beloved fathers, mothers, and children that won't be able to see the holidays.

Via self-driving cars, presumably those deaths and injuries will be a lot less, since the AI won't be prone to drinking and driving, and won't be distracted using a smartphone, etc.

As you can see, driverless cars bode well for making the holidays a time for family and friends to come together and ease the burden of driving, along with making it feasible for people to avert many of the unfortunate adverse consequences of car driving.

Conclusion

In case you are reading this to your children as a bedtime story akin to 'Twas night before Christmas and they are perhaps worried that maybe Santa is going to ditch his reindeer and use instead a driverless sleigh, I assure you that Santa has fully committed to keeping those reindeer.

Yes, St. Nick is going to keep on exclaiming to Dasher, Dancer, Prancer, Vixen, Comet, Cupid, Donner, and Blitzen that they need to dash away, dash away all.

For the kids that are particularly smarmy, they might crack a wee smile and whisper that the reindeer are all robots and AI-based, but don't let them get away with this, and tell them that the reindeer are real and the prancing and pawing of each little hoof are genuine.

And that's the merry and rosy truth on the matter!

CHAPTER 5

AI ON-THE-FLY LEARNING
AND
AI SELF-DRIVING CARS

CHAPTER 5

AI ON-THE-FLY LEARNING

AND

AI SELF-DRIVING CARS

Humans typically learn new things on-the-fly.

Let's use jigsaw puzzles to explore the learning process.

Imagine that you are asked to solve a jigsaw puzzle and you've not previously had the time nor inclination to solve jigsaw puzzles (yes, there are some people that swear they will never do a jigsaw puzzle, as though it is beneath them or otherwise a useless use of their mind).

Upon dumping out onto the table all the pieces from the box, you likely turn all the pieces right side up and do a quick visual scan of the pieces and the picture shown on the box of what you are trying to solve for.

Most people are self-motivated to try and put all the pieces together as efficiently as they can, meaning that it would be unusual for someone to purposely find pieces that fit together and yet not put them together. Reasonable people would be aiming to increasingly build toward solving the jigsaw puzzle and strive to do so in a relatively efficient manner.

A young child is bound to just jump into the task and pick pieces at random, trying to fit them together, even if the colors don't match and even if the shapes don't connect with each other. After a bit of time doing this, most children gradually realize that they ought to be looking to connect pieces that will fit together and that also matches in color as depicted on the overall picture being solved for.

All right, you've had a while to solve the jigsaw puzzle and let's assume you were able to do so.

Did you learn anything in the process of solving the jigsaw puzzle, especially something that might be applied to doing additional jigsaw puzzles later on?

Perhaps you figured out that there are some pieces that are at the edge of the puzzle. Those pieces are easy to find since they have a square edge. Furthermore, you might also divine that if you put together all the edges first, you'll have an outline of the solved puzzle and can build within that outline.

It seems like a smart idea.

In recap, you cleverly noticed a pattern among the pieces, namely that there was some with a straight or squared edge. Based on that pattern, you took an additional mental step and decided that you could likely do the edge of the puzzle with less effort than the rest of the puzzle, plus by completing the overall edge it would seem to further your efforts toward completing the rest of the puzzle.

Maybe you figured this out while doing the puzzle and opted to try the approach right away, rather than simply mentally filing the discovered technique away to use on a later occasion.

I next give you a second jigsaw puzzle.

What do you do?

You might decide to use your newfound technique and proceed ahead by doing the edges first.

Suppose though that I've played a bit of a trick and given you a so-called edgeless jigsaw puzzle. An edgeless version is one that doesn't have a straight or square edge to the puzzle and instead the "edges" are merely everyday pieces that appear to be perpetually unconnected.

If you are insistent on trying to first find all the straight or square-edged pieces, you'll be quite disappointed and frustrated, having to then abandon the edge-first algorithm that you've devised.

Some edgeless puzzles go further by having some pieces that are within the body of the puzzle that have square or straight edges, thereby possibly fooling you into believing that those pieces are for the true edge of the jigsaw.

Overall, here's what happened as you learned to do jigsaw puzzles.

You likely started by doing things in a somewhat random way, especially for the first jigsaw, finding pieces that fit together and assembling portions or chunks of the jigsaw. While doing so, you had noticed that there were some that appeared to be the edges and so you came up with the notion that doing the edges was a keen way to more efficiently solve the puzzle. You might have employed this discovery right away, while in the act of solving the puzzle.

When you were given the second jigsaw, you tried to apply your lesson learned from the first one, but it didn't hold true.

Turns out that the edge approach doesn't always work, though you did not perhaps realize this limitation upon initial discovery of the tactic.

As this quick example showcases, learning can occur in the act of performing a task and might well be helpful for future performances of the task.

Meanwhile, what you've learned during a given task won't necessarily be applicable in future tasks, and could at times confuse you or make you less efficient, since you might be determined to apply something that you've learned and yet it no longer is applicable in other situations.

Adaptive Versus Lockdown While Learning

Learning that occurs on-the-fly is considered adaptive, implying that you are adapting as you go along.

In contrast, if you aren't aiming to learn on-the-fly, you can try to lock out the learning process and seek to proceed without doing any learning. This kind of lockdown of the learning process involves inhibiting any learning and making use of only what has previously been learned.

Voila, now it's time to discuss Artificial Intelligence (AI).

Today's AI systems have seemingly gotten pretty good at a number of human-like tasks (though quite constrained tasks), partially as a result of advances in Machine Learning (ML).

Machine Learning involves the computer system seeking to find patterns and then leveraging those patterns for boosting the performance of the AI.

An AI developer usually opts to try out different kinds of Machine Learning methods when they are putting together an AI system and typically settles on a specific ML that they will then embed into their AI system.

A looming issue that society is gradually uncovering involves whether AI Machine Learning should be adaptive as it performs its efforts, or whether it is better to lockdown the adaptiveness while the ML is undertaking a task.

Let's consider why this an important point.

Such a concern has been specially raised in the MedTech space, involving AI-based medical devices and systems that are being used in medicine and healthcare.

Suppose that an inventor creates a new medical device that examines blood samples and the device while using AI tries to make predictions about the health of the patient that provided the blood.

Usually, such devices would require federal regulatory approval before it could be placed into the marketplace for usage.

If this medical device is making use of AI Machine Learning, it implies that the system could be using adaptive techniques and therefore will try to improve its predictive capability while examining blood samples.

Any federal agency that initially tested the medical device to try and ensure that it was reliable and accurate prior to it being released would have done so at a point in time prior to those adaptive acts that are going to occur while the AI ML is in everyday use.

Thus, the medical device using AI ML is going to inevitably change what it does, likely veering outside the realm of what the agency thought it was approving.

On the downside, the ML is potentially going to "learn" things that aren't necessarily applicable, and yet not realize that those aspects are not always relevant and proceed thusly to falsely assess a given blood sample (recall the story of believing that doing the edge of a jigsaw can be done by simply finding the straight or squared pieces, which didn't turn out to be a valid approach in all cases).

On the upside, the ML might be identifying valuable nuances by being adaptive and self-improve itself toward assessing blood samples, boosting what it does and enhancing patient care.

Yes, some argue, there is that chance of the upside, but when making potentially life-or-death assessments, do we want an AI Machine Learning algorithm being "unleashed" such that it could adapt in ways that aren't desirable and might, in fact, be downright dangerous?

That's the rub.

Some assert that the adaptive aspects should not be allowed on-the-fly to adjust what the AI system does, and instead in a lockdown mode merely collect and identify potential changes that they would be inspected and approved by a human, such as the AI developers that put together the system.

Furthermore, in a regulatory situation, the AI developers would need to go back to the regulatory agency and propose that the AI system is now a newly proposed updated version and get agency approval before those adaptations were used in the real-world acts of the system.

This thorny question about adaptiveness running free or being locked down is often called "the update problem" and is raising quite a debate.

In case you think the answer is simple, always lockdown, unfortunately, life is not always so easy.

Those that don't want the lockdown are apt to say that doing so will hamstring the AI Machine Learning, which presumably has the advantage of being able to self-adjust and get better as it undertakes its efforts.

If you force the AI ML to perform in a lockdown manner, you might as well toss out the AI ML since it no longer is free to adjust and enhance what it does.

Trying to find a suitable middle ground, some suggest that there could be guardrails that serve to keep the AI ML from going too far astray.

By putting boundaries or limits on the kinds of adjustments or adaptiveness, you could maybe get the best of both worlds, namely a form of adaptive capability that furthers the system and yet keeps it within a suitable range that won't cause the system to seemingly become unsavory.

The U.S. Food and Drug Administration (FDA) has sketched a regulatory framework for AI ML and medical devices that is seeking input on this "update problem" debate.

Overall, this element of AI ML is still up for debate across all areas of application, not just the medical domain, and brings to the forefront the tradeoffs involved in deploying AI ML systems.

Here's an interesting question: *Do we want true self-driving cars to be able to utilize AI Machine Learning in an adaptive manner or in a lockdown manner?*

It's kind of a trick question or at least a tricky question.

Let's unpack the matter.

The Levels Of Self-Driving Cars

It is important to clarify what I mean when referring to true self-driving cars.

True self-driving cars are ones that the AI drives the car entirely on its own and there isn't any human assistance during the driving task.

These driverless vehicles are considered a Level 4 and Level 5, while a car that requires a human driver to co-share the driving effort is usually considered at a Level 2 or Level 3.

The cars that co-share the driving task are described as being semi-autonomous, and typically contain a variety of automated add-on's that are referred to as ADAS (Advanced Driver-Assistance Systems).

There is not yet a true self-driving car at Level 5, which we don't yet even know if this will be possible to achieve, and nor how long it will take to get there.

Meanwhile, the Level 4 efforts are gradually trying to get some traction by undergoing very narrow and selective public roadway trials, though there is controversy over whether this testing should be allowed per se (we are all life-or-death guinea pigs in an experiment taking place on our highways and byways, some point out).

Since semi-autonomous cars require a human driver, the adoption of those types of cars won't be markedly different than driving conventional vehicles, so I'm not going to include them in this discussion about AI ML (though for clarification, Level 2 and Level 3 could indeed have AI ML involved in their systems and thus this discussion overall is relevant even to semi-autonomous cars).

For semi-autonomous cars, it is equally important that I mention a disturbing aspect that's been arising, namely that in spite of those human drivers that keep posting videos of themselves falling asleep at the wheel of a Level 2 or Level 3 car, we all need to avoid being misled into believing that the driver can take away their attention from the driving task while driving a semi-autonomous car.

You are the responsible party for the driving actions of the vehicle, regardless of how much automation might be tossed into a Level 2 or Level 3.

Self-Driving Cars And Update Problem

For Level 4 and Level 5 true self-driving vehicles, there won't be a human driver involved in the driving task.

All occupants will be passengers.

The AI is doing the driving.

The AI driving software is developed, tested, and loaded into the on-board computer processors that are in the driverless car. To allow for the AI software to be updated over time, the driverless car has an OTA (Over-The-Air) electronic communication capability.

When the AI developers decide its time to do an update, they will push out the latest version of the AI driving software to the vehicle. Usually, this happens while the self-driving car is parked, say in your garage, perhaps charging up if it's an EV, and the OTA then takes place.

Right now, it is rare for the OTA updating to occur while the car is in motion, though there are efforts underway for enabling OTA of that nature (I'll explain the controversy about this momentarily).

Not only can updates be pushed into the driverless car, the OTA can be used to grab up aspects from the self-driving car. For example, the sensors on the self-driving car will have collected lots of images, video, and radar and LIDAR data, doing so during a driving journey. This data could be sent up to the cloud being used by the automaker or self-driving tech firm.

We are ready now to discuss the AI Machine Learning topic as it relates to adaptiveness versus lockdown in the use case of self-driving cars.

Should the AI ML that's on-board the driverless car be allowed to update itself, being adaptive, or should the updates only be performed via OTA from the cloud and as based on presumably the latest updates instituted and approved by the AI developers?

Consider the instance of a driverless car that encounters a dog in the roadway.

Perhaps the AI ML on-board the self-driving car detects the dog and opts to honk the horn of the car to try and prod the dog to get out of the way.

Let's pretend that the horn honking succeeds and the dog scampers away.

In an adaptive mode, the AI ML might adjust to now include that honking the horn is successful at prompting an animal to get off the road.

Suppose a while later, there's a cat in the road. The AI system opts to honk the horn, and the cat scurries away.

So far, this horn honking seems to be working out well.

The next day, there's a moose in the roadway.

The AI system honks the horn, since doing so worked previously, and assumes the moose is going to run away.

Oops, turns out that the moose opts to charge toward the driverless car, having been startled by the horn and decides that it should charge at the menacing mechanical beast.

Now, I realize this example is a bit contrived, but I'm trying to quickly illustrate that the AI ML of an adaptive style could adjust in a manner that won't necessarily be right in all cases (again, recall the earlier jigsaw story).

Rather than the on-board AI ML adjusting, perhaps it would be safer to keep it in lockdown.

But, you say, the onboard AI will be forever in a static state and not be improving.

Well, recall that there's the OTA capability of updating.

Presumably, the driverless car could have provided the data about the initial instance of the dog and the horn honking up to the cloud, and the AI developers might have studied the matter.

Then, upon carefully adjusting the AI system, the AI developers might, later on, push the latest animal avoidance routine down into the driverless car.

The point being that there is an open question about whether we want to have multi-ton life-or-death cars on our roadways that are being run by AI that is able to adjust itself, or whether we want the onboard AI to be on lockdown and only allow updates via OTA (which presumably would be explicitly derived and approved via human hands and minds).

That's the crux of the "update problem" for driverless cars.

Conclusion

There is a plethora of tradeoffs involved in the self-driving car adaptiveness dilemma.

If a self-driving car isn't adjusting on-the-fly, it might not cope well with any new situations that crop-up and will perhaps fail to make an urgent choice appropriately. Having to wait maybe hours, days, or weeks to get an OTA update might prolong the time that the AI continues to be unable to adequately handle certain roadway situations.

Human drivers adapt on-the-fly, and if we are seeking to have the AI driving system be as good or possibly better than human drivers, wouldn't we want and need to have the AI ML be adaptive on-the-fly?

Can suitable system-related guardrails be put in place to keep the AI ML from adapting in some kind of wild or untoward manner?

Though we commonly deride human drivers for their flaws and foibles, the ability of humans to learn and adjust their behavior is quite a marvel, one that continues to be somewhat elusive when it comes to achieving the same in AI and Machine Learning.

Some believe that we need to solve the jigsaw puzzle of the human mind and how it works before we'll have AI ML that's of any top form.

This isn't a mere edge problem and instead sits at the core of achieving true AI.

.

CHAPTER 6
LEVEL 4 AND LEVEL 5 OF AI SELF-DRIVING CARS

CHAPTER 6

LEVEL 4 AND LEVEL 5 OF
AI SELF-DRIVING CARS

What's a Level 4 or Level 5 self-driving car?

One of the most popular questions asked about self-driving cars involves the various levels of automation that constitute a self-driving car. Those levels range from a rank or score of 0 to 5, consisting of Level 0 as being the least amount of automation and then raising at each level until topping out at Level 5 as the most automation.

Not only is it a popular question, but the levels of automation are also one of the largest sources of confusion about self-driving cars.

People often have generally heard about the levels of self-driving cars and yet are unsure of what each of the levels designates.

The media frequently makes things worse by misstating the nature of the levels, or by using the levels in misleading ways that are not in keeping with the proper definition of the levels. Sadly, sometimes a fake news article about self-driving cars will pretend that there is no formal definition of the levels or decide to make-up their own definition entirely.

Truly sad.

I'd like to set the record straight.

There is, in fact, a published standard that depicts the automation levels and it has become a well-worn and oft-cited cornerstone to discussing and understanding self-driving cars, though primarily only used by insiders within the self-driving car industry and less so used by non-insiders.

Part of the reason that non-insiders tend to refrain from making use of the standard is due to the somewhat technical or wonky writing style.

Rightfully, a key standard that is at the core of defining levels of automation is bound to be relatively technical, suitably so for the purposes of the document to stand as useful as a relatively precise and exacting document.

The shorthand notation by insiders to refer to the standard is to say that it is SAE J3016.

Let's unpack that notation.

This standards document is one of many promulgated by the SAE (Society of Automotive Engineers).

To easily refer to the numerous standards associated with automobiles and other types of vehicles, they are each assigned a numbered reference.

The one that focuses on the automation levels for self-driving cars has the designation of J3016.

Thus, the quickest way to refer to the standard is by simply uttering SAE J3016.

You are now becoming an insider!

Overview Of The Levels

The SAE J3016 has a somewhat lofty and technical title of "Taxonomy and Definitions for Terms Related to Driving Automation Systems for On-Road Motor Vehicles" and fits within the rubric of the Surface Vehicle Recommended Practice aspects.

I'm not going to cover the levels that require the presence of a human driver, which are Level 0, Level 1, Level 2, and Level 3.

By-and-large, those lower levels of automation are rather self-apparent and involve having automation that augments a human driver.

Cars that require a human driver will often co-share the driving task, meaning that human drivers and automation of the car are supposed to work hand-in-hand while driving the car. These types of cars are properly described as being semi-autonomous vehicles rather than autonomous vehicles (AVs), and typically contain a variety of automated add-on's that are known as ADAS (Advanced Driver-Assistance Systems).

Since semi-autonomous cars require a human driver, the adoption of those types of cars won't be markedly different than driving conventional vehicles, so I'm not going to include Level 0 to Level 3 in this discussion.

For semi-autonomous cars, it is equally important that I mention a disturbing aspect that's been arising, namely that in spite of those human drivers that keep posting videos of themselves falling asleep at the wheel of a Level 2 or Level 3 car, we all need to avoid being misled into believing that the driver can take away their attention from the driving task while driving a semi-autonomous car.

You are the responsible party for the driving actions of the vehicle, regardless of how much automation might be tossed into a Level 2 or Level 3.

You might be wondering which vehicles today are at which level of automation.

As an example, existing Tesla's are considered at a Level 2 and are gradually via the expansion of AutoPilot becoming closer to Level 3.

Meanwhile, Waymo and many others are aiming at Level 4 and Level 5 (I mention just Waymo because they are generally accepted as the furthest along on such efforts and are also widely known among the public, but there are plenty of other Level 4 and Level 5 efforts underway).

When referring to Level 4 and Level 5, I've found it handy to refer to those topmost levels as being true self-driving cars.

True self-driving cars are ones that Artificial Intelligence (AI) drives the car entirely on its own and there isn't any human assistance required during the driving task.

There is not yet a true self-driving car at Level 5, which we don't yet even know if this will be possible to achieve, and nor how long it will take to get there.

Meanwhile, the Level 4 efforts are gradually trying to get some traction by undergoing very narrow and selective public roadway trials, though there is controversy over whether this testing should be allowed per se (we are all life-or-death guinea pigs in an experiment taking place on our highways and byways, some point out).

I'm guessing you are likely curious to know more about how Level 4 and Level 5 are the same and how they differ, so let's jump further into the details.

Self-Driving Cars And The Role Of Human Drivers

For Level 4 and Level 5 true self-driving vehicles, there won't necessarily be a human driver involved in the driving task.

This is what makes them so special and catches our attention and interest.

We've all seen science fiction movies that have cars that drive via AI only (no human driver), and it's quite a promising technical achievement, along with freeing humans from having to know how to drive or arrange for a human driver when wanting to use a car.

Many hope that human driverless cars, which I'm referring to as true self-driving cars, will bring forth mobility-for-all, enabling those that are mobility disadvantaged or mobility marginally to finally have ready access to riding in cars.

This discussion about human drivers brings up one source of confusion about Level 4 and Level 5.

The formal definition says that there is no requirement that a human driver <u>must</u> be available for a Level 4 and nor for a Level 5 self-driving car.

Take a moment to reflect upon that use of the word "must" and you'll realize that just because you might say that something doesn't have to happen, it does not preclude allowing it to happen.

In other words, automakers and self-driving tech firms are able to decide to allow for human drivers to function inside a Level 4 or Level 5 self-driving car, if wishing to do so.

Perhaps a particular self-driving car might have driving controls included for humans that might want to drive the self-driving car, choosing to do so whenever they might please. Likewise, if the self-driving car does have human accessible driving controls, the AI might decide to hand over the driving to the human driver, assuming that a human driver happens to be present in the car at the time of seeking to do the handoff (another provision would be to allow for remote drivers).

There is a rub to this.

If you believe that the AI will be a safer driver than human drivers, presumably due to the aspect that the AI won't drive drunk and otherwise drive in human faltering ways, you would aim to intentionally prevent human drivers from being able to drive.

By opening the door to the notion of allowing humans to drive a Level 4 or Level 5, a true self-driving car is said to potentially open a Pandora's box.

As such, many are intending to remove driver controls from within true self-driving cars.

This would not only inhibit a human driver from trying to take over the driving from the AI, it also frees up the interior of the car to be redesigned. For example, future designs of such cars showcase that without the need for a steering wheel and pedals, you can reconfigure the interior, perhaps having swivel seats or reclining seats to allow passengers to take a nap while riding in a self-driving car.

There are valid reasons to consider allowing for human driving at Level 4 and Level 5.

Suppose the on-board AI system becomes messed-up or frozen, perhaps due to a car accident that involves getting rear-ended and harms the computer processors, and there's no means to now drive the car.

How will someone get the self-driving car off the roadway and out of traffic when it has become a multi-ton deadweight without any driving capacity?

The human driving controls aspects is a tradeoff that is still being debated.

In short, true self-driving cars at Level 4 or Level 5:

- Are not required to allow for human driving

- Are not required to disallow human driving

- May allow human driving to occur if the automaker wishes to include it

- Some worry that allowing for human driving is a bad idea

- Removal of driving controls also offers to free up space inside the car

- Automakers and self-driving tech makers are allowed flexibility in this regard

Key Difference In Level 4 Versus Level 5

Okay, so both Level 4 and Level 5 are about being driverless, though this is not a hard-and-fast rule since the maker of such self-driving cars can opt to allow for human driving.

Next, let's consider what is decidedly the biggest and most important difference between Level 4 and Level 5.

It has to do with the scope of where and when a true self-driving car is going to drive.

Let's ponder scope aspects.

Suppose you are trying to invent a new kind of screwdriver.

You work on it and are able to make it work on screws that have a flat or slotted top. That's great, but it won't yet work on screws that have a crosshead, known as Phillips.

Is the screwdriver useful even though it can't yet handle crosshead screws?

Sure, the screwdriver is still handy, though its scope is narrow, and you'd like to somehow have the screwdriver be functional for crosshead screws too.

Maybe devising a screwdriver that can handle both types of screws is hard to figure out.

Indeed, perhaps you come up with a second screwdriver that is devoted to crosshead screws, and thus now have two screwdrivers.

Notice that both types of screwdrivers have the same overarching purpose, yet for now, they are each of their own types.

Your hope is to someday produce one screwdriver that can handle all types of screws, including flat top, Phillips, and even others like hex key, etc.

What does this have to do with Level 4 and Level 5 self-driving cars?

Level 5 is easy to understand, it is essentially a true self-driving car that can go anywhere and at any time, assuming that a human driver could do the same.

I mention the caveat that the Level 5 goes wherever and whenever a human driver could do the same since we aren't going to require the Level 5 to go beyond what humans could do in terms of reasonably driving a car.

For example, if a human driver can't drive a car across an unnavigable rushing stream, it's not fair to assume that the AI could do so since as a driving task the driving effort has to do with being able to drive the car in reasonable ways. Adding AI to a car doesn't mean it can magically fly or leap across an otherwise unnavigable rushing stream.

Level 5 is what most people have in their minds when you tell them that true self-driving cars are going to one day be on our roadways.

How does Level 4 differ?

Level 4 is like the screwdrivers that I early mentioned, namely that for Level 4 true self-driving cars there is a scope that an automaker or self-driving tech firm can impose upon the drivability of the AI.

One automaker might make a Level 4 self-driving car that works within downtown San Francisco and only functions in sunny weather. That's the scope, similar to saying that you have a screwdriver that works on flat head screws, but not on other types of screws.

Thus, this particular Level 4 self-driving car won't work when you decide to take it to say Los Angeles (which is outside the scope of San Francisco).

Or, it won't work in San Francisco if it is a rainy day (since this is outside the scope of sunny weather).

It is "easier" to make a Level 4 than a Level 5, for the same reason that it is easier to make a series of differing screwdrivers for different situations than it is to have a universal one.

Nearly everyone in the Level 4 and Level 5 game is starting with developing Level 4, and then hoping to gradually expand and extend the Level 4 into becoming a Level 5.

Level 5 though is a tall order.

Humans are actually quite capable drivers overall, being able to drive a car in sunny weather, in rainy weather, in snow, and in cities, and in suburbs, and in many other circumstances.

The path to Level 5 seems to be a divide-and-conquer approach, let's do narrowly scoped uses, and eventually turn this into the all-encompassing multi-use tool.

These scopes that I'm alluding to are formally called ODD (Operational Design Domain).

Here's a quote from the standard that helps indicate the Level 4 versus Level 5 capabilities of the Automated Driving System (ADS):

- Level 4: "Permits engagement only within its ODD"

- Level 5: "Permits engagement of the ADS under all driver-manageable on-road conditions"

Here's the formal definition of ODD:

- "Operating conditions under which a given driving automation system or feature thereof is specifically designed to function, including, but not limited to, environmental, geographical, and time-of-day restrictions, and/or the requisite presence or absence of certain traffic or roadway characteristics."

These ODD's can be whatever an automaker or self-driving tech firm decides it should be, such as saying that their self-driving car won't work at nighttime and only during the day. Meanwhile, some other automaker offers a self-driving car that will work during nighttime and daytime, but maybe it won't work in the rain.

It is confusing to the public and the media that these ODD's aren't defined in a standardized way.

In other words, an automaker or self-driving tech firm can decide to divine their own proprietary ODD's.

This means that if you see a self-driving car driving past you, there's no immediate way to know what its scope consists of.

Maybe it has been devised to go only in a 10-block radius of where you happen to see it, or maybe it can go across your state to other cities. Perhaps it can work in the rain, but not in snow. And so on.

For self-driving cars that are going to be used for ridesharing, you'll have no direct means of knowing what the scope of that self-driving car might be.

Presumably, hopefully, at least whoever owns the self-driving car will make available the scope limitations, perhaps stating as such when you request a ridesharing pick-up involving a self-driving car.

In recap:

- Level 4 is a self-driving car that has some kind of bounded scope of where and when it will drive

- The bounded scope is formally called its ODD (Operational Design Domain)

- There is no standardized set of ODD's and thus they can vary by automaker or tech maker

- Level 5 has no bounded scope per se and thus essentially encompasses all feasible ODD's

- Both Level 4 and Level 5 are allowed to be limited to what is humanly drivable

- All the levels of the standard, including Level 4 and Level 5, apply only to on-road driving and thus off-road driving is not a requirement by the standard

Conclusion

For those readers that know the SAE J3016 by heart, you'll notice that I've tried to simplify the language used to describe the levels of automation, and as a result, the herein description is not quite as precise as the actual standard, though nonetheless provides a fair, readable, and accurate depiction.

Those of you that were paying close attention, you might have noticed that there is an important and somewhat hidden and unheralded phrase that came up in the levels of automation, namely the indication of off-road versus on-road.

Many don't realize that the SAE J3016 considers the standard to apply to on-road driving and does not necessarily apply to off-road driving.

Here's the definition of on-road:
- "On-road refers to publicly accessible roadways (including parking areas and private campuses that permit public access) that collectively serve users of vehicles of all classes and driving automation levels (including no driving automation), as well as motorcyclists, pedal cyclists, and pedestrians."

Ponder this important nuance.

As mentioned, Level 4 and Level 5 involve driving acts that are human drivers feasible, but there is a caveat to that aspect.

The definition caveat is that it includes only on-road driving and excludes, therefore, off-road driving (though, presumably off-road driving is another one of those optional additions).

Human drivers can drive off-road, there's no doubt about that.

The definition for Level 4 and Level 5 is only with respect to humans being able to drive on-road.

Few realize that this limitation or constraint exists in the standard.

If you have the time to do so, you ought to consider reading the entire SAE J3016 document, especially for those interested in self-driving cars. There are lots of twists and turns included, and I assure you it is as engaging as reading a mystery story or drama novella.

Self-driving cars are going to undeniably impact our society.

It is therefore crucial that we all be sufficiently informed, and make sure that when you refer to a rose, it is a rose, and not something else since our words do matter and what we mean by them is vital to discussion and understanding.

CHAPTER 7

EXPLAINING KEY ACRONYMS AND AI SELF-DRIVING CARS

CHAPTER 7

EXPLAINING KEY ACRONYMS AND AI SELF-DRIVING CARS

When you go to see your medical doctor, they sometimes use medical jargon that is hard to understand and leaves you feeling unsure and unable to engage in a lively discussion about your medical condition.

Most professions have their own set of lingo and specialized acronyms, providing a kind of shortcut way to express aspects in their specialty.

Anthropologists point out that besides using language as a shorthand, the vocabulary of specialists in a particular domain provides a cultural way of fitting in among fellow experts. Indeed, sometimes an expert will purposely brandish their lingo as a means of showboating and serve as a form of puffery.

If you try to dig into the lingo of a profession, the vocab frequently includes seemingly inscrutable alphabet soup-like acronyms.

It's hard enough to grasp the meaning of one acronym, let alone make sense of them when the acronyms are stacked up one after another, turning a sentence into a scree of capital letters and appearing to be a strange foreign language.

To be clear, any such vocabulary does serve a quite useful purpose.

One vital purpose consists of being able to have coherent discourse, trying to ensure that if one person speaks of a rose, others all have an in-common understanding of what the word rose means. If one expert assumes that a rose means a rose, while a fellow colleague thinks a rose means an apple, the odds are that any discussion will breakdown right away as neither one agrees with the other.

The definitions of the vocabulary words, phrases, and acronyms in a domain are crucial since otherwise everyone is talking past each other and inexorable confusion will result.

Self-Driving Car Industry Jargon

The self-driving car industry is replete with numerous acronyms and specialized lingo.

Here's a taste of some of the oft used acronyms: ADS, ODD, DDT, OEDR, OTA, V2X, ADAS, etc.

If you know what each of those means, kudos!

If you think maybe you know what each of those means, tip of the hat for your awareness.

If you don't know what they mean or have heard or seen them but aren't quite sure what they mean, welcome to the club since most people are in that same boat.

Now, some of the jargon associated with self-driving cars have relatively crisp definitions, but there is much lingo that is not well defined and remains elusive.

Unfortunately, the elusive portion tends to allow the media to use the lingo in ways that industry insiders find disquieting or downright upsetting.

Pile on top that even the well-defined vocab is repeatedly misrepresented by the media, including distorting the meaning or changing the meaning by using the lingo in ways that aren't the intended use, and we've got a colossal communications mess on our hands.

A rose becomes an apple which becomes a gorilla.

How can the public be expected to realize what the true state of self-driving cars consists of, and where it is heading, when the words expressed are so sloppily bandied about?

How can regulators aim to provide suitable regulatory guidelines and rules if the meaning of the words and phrases of the industry are malleable and shapeless?

It's a problem.

Part of the basis for the difficulty in assigning distinct and inarguable meaning to the lingo is that the field is generally new and evolving.

Unlike other professions that have had a long time to iron out their wording issues, the field of self-driving cars is relatively young and immature.

That's not to say that there aren't plentiful efforts underway to pin down the jargon.

There are.

I'll be providing herein what I believe to be a consensus and informal style definition for many of the most commonly used acronyms and words, along with including some of the formalized versions of the definitions (especially citing what many consider the well-accepted definitions that are being promulgated by the Society of Automotive Engineers or SAE, and as especially reflected in the SAE J3016 standard).

There are those insiders that might have some heartburn with my informal definitions, and indeed there are insiders that already have heartburn over the formalized definitions too.

The hope here is to provide a semblance of what the vocab consists of, aiding all readers to come up-to-speed, and engage all in a dialogue about what the meaning is, could be, and ought to be.

That's the caveat to keep in mind as you read the definitions.

A dictionary lists words in alphabetical order, which is handy since you can then quickly find a word by looking for it in its proper sequence.

Rather than using a dictionary sequencing approach, I'll cover the jargon in a sequence that gradually builds upon each of the acronyms and phrases, doing so in a somewhat logical manner rather than a strictly alphabetic order. This will be more readily comprehensible and provide a gradual, progressive sense of order.

Trying to keep the list succinct, not all acronyms and not all words and phrases are being included. It is admittedly a cherry-picking of the most commonly used and relied upon ones.

With no further ado, let's unpack the matter.

Untangling What We Shall Call A Self-Driving Car

The best place to start this jargon journey consists of the very cornerstone of how to say that you are referring to self-driving cars.

It's an unsightly problem when everybody willy-nilly opts to use whatever phrases they wish when denoting an entire thing or field of inquiry (let alone the subordinated words and phrases).

Here are various ways that people refer to self-driving cars:
- Self-Driving Car
- Driverless Car
- Autonomous Car
- Robo-Car (also Robo-Taxi)
- Autonomous Vehicle (AV)
- Semi-Autonomous Vehicle
- Advanced Driver Assistance System (ADAS)
- Automated Driving System (ADS)
- Etc.

A wealth of riches in terminology, yet indubitably bankrupt since it is too loosey-goosey.

My preference and the preference by most that have considered the matter studiously is to normally use the phrase "self-driving cars" when referring to cars that are outfitted with automation that makes them able to drive without human intervention. It seems sensible to use because the "self-driving" portion implies that the car is able to drive itself, which is a handy and apt implication.

The phrase "driverless car" is somewhat problematic because it presumes that the word "driverless" is referring to the aspect that there isn't a human driver, though the word "driverless" can also have a double meaning and imply that nothing at all is driving the car, which doesn't make any sense since the automation is indeed doing the driving.

Presumably, the phrase "autonomous car" might be a better choice since it contains the word "autonomous" and therefore directly implies that the car is being driven by the automation, but it isn't as catchy and seems flat on the tongue.

One of the most detested phrases is "robo-car" since it suggests that a robot is sitting in the driver's seat and driving the car, though that's not the path being primarily pursued (there are some efforts along those lines, though they are far and few between).

The close cousin to robo-car is robo-taxi which is even worse since it not only has the same robot-implying element it also uses the word "taxi" and suggests that all self-driving cars will be used on a ridesharing basis (perhaps most will, but not necessarily all).

Researchers tend to use the phrase "autonomous vehicle" and its corresponding acronym of AV, though this is not seemingly as well-accepted by the general populace, plus the word "vehicles" is a broad term that encompasses cars, trucks, boats, submarines, drones, planes, and the like. Thus, using AV is not specific and makes it less useful if you are desirous of referring solely to self-driving cars.

On a related note, keep in mind that a car can be fully autonomous, or it can be partially autonomous (meaning that there is a human driver required and the automation supplements the human driver), which adds confusion to the matter and makes the wording additionally problematic.

The phrase "semi-autonomous car" helps somewhat to clarify that you are referring to a car that is less automated and thus presumably not a fully autonomous or true self-driving car.

Similarly, ADAS or Advanced Drivers Assistance System is indicative that the automation is intended to assist a human driver, rather than replace the human driver.

ADS or Automated Driving System is the formal terminology used by the SAE to refer to the driving system that covers levels 3 to 5 of the taxonomy of driving automation (I'll explain the levels momentarily):

- *ADS (Automated Driving System)*

- Formal definition: "The hardware and software that are collectively capable of performing the entire dynamic driving task (DDT) on a sustained basis, regardless of whether it is limited to a specific operational design domain (ODD)."

Talking About Driving

This brings us then to the next logical juncture of wanting to define the levels of automation for driving, along with explaining what DDT and ODD are about.

Let's start with DDT or the dynamic driving task, which boiled down means driving the car:

- *DDT (Dynamic Driving Task)*
-
- Formal definition: "All of the real-time operational and tactical functions required to operate a vehicle in on-road traffic, excluding the strategic functions such as trip scheduling and selection of destinations and waypoints."

The ODD or operational design domain has to do with where and when the driving automation is capable of driving the car or its defined scope:

- *ODD (Operational Design Domain)*

- Formal definition: "Operating conditions under which a given driving automation system or feature thereof is specifically designed to function, including but not limited to, environmental, geographical, and time-of-day restrictions, and/or the requisite presence or absence of certain traffic or roadway characteristics."

And the levels of driving automation are used to denote how capable the driving automation is, ranging from a score or rank of 0 to a topmost score of 5 (with the topmost score meaning the fullest capable).

- *Level 0: No Driving Automation*

- Formal definition: "The performance by the driver of the entire dynamic driving task, even when enhanced by active safety systems."

- *Level 1: Driver Assistance*

- Formal definition: "The sustained and operational design domain-specific execution by a driving automation system of either the lateral or the longitudinal vehicle motion control subtask of the dynamic driving task (but not both simultaneously) with the expectation that the driver performs the remainder of the DDT."

- *Level 2: Partial Driving Automation*

- Formal definition: "The sustained and operational design domain-specific execution by a driving automation system of both the lateral and longitudinal vehicle motion control subtasks of the dynamic driving task with the expectation that the driver completes the object and event detection and response subtask and supervises the driving automation system."

- *Level 3: Conditional Driving Automation*

- Formal definition: "The sustained and operational design domain-specific performance by an automated driving system of the entire dynamic driving task with the expectation that the dynamic driving task fallback-ready user is receptive to an automated driving system issued requests to intervene, as well as to dynamic driving task performance relevant system failures in other vehicle systems, and will respond appropriately."

- *Level 4: High Driving Automation*

- Formal definition: "The sustained and operational design domain-specific performance by an automated driving system of the entire dynamic driving task and dynamic driving task fallback without any expectation that a user will respond to a request to intervene."

- *Level 5: Full Driving Automation*

- Formal definition: "The sustained and unconditional (i.e., not operational design domain-specific) performance by an automated driving system of the entire dynamic driving task and dynamic driving task fallback without any expectation that a user will respond to a request to intervene."

In recap, there are lots of ways to refer to self-driving cars, of which the preference when mentioning a car that has automation allowing the car to drive itself is the phrase "self-driving cars" and then if the car requires a human driver it is referred to as a "semi-autonomous car" or one that is using ADAS (Advanced Driver Assistance System).

The act of driving is referred to as the DDT or dynamic driving task, and for establishing a scope of where the automation is capable of driving, such as say only with a specific city and only in daylight, it is the designated ODD or operational design domain.

And, we use the score of 0 to 5 to denote how capable the automation is, seeking to achieve the vaunted topmost score of 5, a fully autonomous car that can drive anywhere and anytime that a human could drive a car.

Lingo About Sensory Aspects

We can now move into the additional territory of phrases and acronyms that go beyond the aforementioned core.

To undertake the driving task, the automation uses various sensory devices such as cameras, radar, ultrasonic, thermal, LIDAR, and so on, which enable the AI to detect what's going on around the car and act somewhat like the eyes and ears of a human driver.

The proper acronym for these automation eyes-and-ears, along with the act of using the collected sensory info to drive the car is OEDR:

- *OEDR (Object and Event Detection and Response)*

- Formal definition: "The subtasks of the dynamic driving task that include monitoring the driving environment (detecting, recognizing, and classifying objects and events and preparing to respond as needed) and executing an appropriate response to such objects and events (i.e., as needed to complete the dynamic driving task and/or dynamic driving task fallback).

A somewhat informal term is used to describe the act of bringing together the sensory collected data and trying to make it into a cohesive whole, usually referred to as sensor fusion:

- *MDSF (Multi-Data Sensor Fusion)*

- Informal definition: The act of bringing together or fusing the sensory data collected from a multitude of sensory devices, doing so during the driving task, along with reconciling conflicts and aligning elements to gain an overarching semblance of the driving scene.

A sensory device known as LIDAR has become quite popular for use on self-driving cars, though there is some controversy in that Tesla and Elon Musk eschew using LIDAR.

- LIDAR (Light Detection And Ranging)

- Informal definition: A sensory device that is considered a mashup of light and radar, which emits a laser light beam and upon reflection attempts to detect the distance between itself and whatever object the light bounces off.

Let's take a breath and mull over this added lingo.

Whenever you hear about or see a self-driving car, one aspect to be looking for consists of the type of sensors being used, along with how the data from those sensors are incorporated into the AI being able to drive the car.

The overall capability is the OEDR, while the sub-portion that deals with bringing together the sensory is the MDSF, and among the myriad of sensors could be the use of LIDAR.

Hopefully, that otherwise cryptic sentence now makes sense to you!

Lingo About Communications

A true self-driving car is intended to be able to work all on its own and not need to communicate with any other external system to figure out how to drive the car.

This is considered a sacrosanct principle being pursued.

But, this doesn't mean that you can't supplement the on-board AI by allowing it to communicate with other external systems that might aid the driving task.

Here are some important terms:

- *Connected Vehicle (CV)*
- Informal definition: A car that has communications capabilities to connect with external systems.

- *V2X (Vehicle-to-everything)*
- Informal definition: A means to allow a vehicle to communicate with a variety of external systems, including for example V2V, V2I, V2P.

- *V2V (Vehicle-to-Vehicle)*
- Informal definition: A means to allow a vehicle to communicate with another vehicle.

- *V2I (Vehicle-to-Infrastructure)*
- Informal definition: A means to allow a vehicle to communicate with roadway infrastructure such as traffic lights, bridges, railroad crossings, etc.

- *V2P (Vehicle-to-Pedestrian)*
- Informal definition: A means to allow a vehicle to electronically communicate with pedestrians.

- *OTA (Over-The-Air)*
- Informal definition: A means to allow a vehicle to communicate with a cloud-based system, enabling the onboard AI to receive updates and allowing the car to push sensory data and other info up to the cloud.

That's quite a mouthful of acronyms.

Here's a quick quiz for you.

See if this sentence makes sense to you:

A self-driving car used it's OTA this morning and got its latest AI updates, and while on a later driving journey used V2V to coordinate with other self-driving cars to coordinate traffic activity, including having avoided a freeway wreck that V2I broadcasted about.

Did the use of OTA, V2V, and V2I make sense?

Hopefully so.

Conclusion

Now for your final exam, try to make sense of this:

The semi-autonomous car using ADAS was not as capable as the Level 4 ADS and lacked the AI needed to autonomously perform the DDT for a complex ODD, partially because the OEDR was insufficient and especially had limited MDSF, along with lacking LIDAR, though it was a CV and could potentially use the OTA to advance, and was equipped too with V2V though not yet able to handle V2P and nor V2I.

Did you get that?

There are many more acronyms and phrases pertinent to self-driving cars, but you've now earned your honorary badge of the self-driving cars 101 and ought to pat yourself on the back accordingly.

CHAPTER 8
WALMART
EDGE COMPUTING AND
AI SELF-DRIVING CARS

CHAPTER 8

WALMART EDGE COMPUTING AND AI SELF-DRIVING CARS

A recent business news story indicates that mighty Walmart is aiming to put in place specialized computers at their stores that would be used to aid self-driving cars presumably needing so-called "edge computing" capabilities.

Say what?

According to the media reports on this somewhat startling revelation, the notion is that self-driving cars that are using the cloud to undertake driving actions will be able to more readily get such computing needs fulfilled by using a nearby computer server sitting at a Walmart versus having to communicate all the way to a potentially far distant cloud-based server.

With Walmart having stores conveniently distributed throughout the U.S., apparently, about 90% of Americans live within 10 miles of a Walmart store, and thus this proposed approach appears to have some merit (kind of).

If you assume that self-driving cars are going to primarily be driving where people are going to be, which certainly seems to make logical sense, the idea of being able to have a self-driving car connect with a nearby computer server and hop electronically from one to the next would seem convenient and a brilliant way to leverage the real estate holdings of Walmart.

Imagine a self-driving car on a journey across your local town or city, and meanwhile, the AI of the driverless vehicle is rapidly pinging and sourcing computer processing cycles while it just so happens to be going past various Walmart's sprinkled here and there.

Little did you realize that your local Walmart is not just selling bananas, frozen foods, low-priced shirts and the like, but apparently you'll be able to save money and live better if that Walmart is also acting as an outsourced data center for roving driverless cars that are in the surrounding area.

At first glance, this might seem like some extraordinarily ingenious insight.

Though we all tend to think of Walmart as a retailer, perhaps it could make some extra bucks off the happenstance that they have over 4,700 brick-and-mortar locations dispersed across the country and especially at high density within the most populated areas (well, of course, this isn't just happenstance since to get people into their stores means the stores have to be nearby where people are).

Imagine a bunch of top executives sitting around a boardroom table and trying to come up with new ways of making money.

If they've already tried all sorts of ways to squeeze more from the retailing side and believe they've gotten as much there as they can for now, maybe a moment of outside-the-box thinking arose that figured out to interplay two upcoming trends, namely the advent of self-driving cars and the emergence of edge computing.

Take those two-promising tech-related innovations and add Walmart into the mixture, voila, you got yourself a potential goldmine mash-up.

Wait a second, if this is such a big money-making approach, maybe somebody ought to be on the phone with some other companies with a similarly widespread physical presence in our populated locales.

There are about 6,200 Starbucks across the U.S. and those are certainly nearby to where people live and travel (and crave their latte and coffees).

That's a whopping score of 6,200 Starbucks locations versus "only" about 4,700 locations for Walmart.

Hold on, McDonald's has about 14,000 locations in the United States.

Cha-ching goes the cash register for McDonald's to do a one-upmanship with their 2x or 3x number of locations and slap in those edge computers.

That though can be easily topped by Subway, coming in at about 24,000 locations from coast to coast.

Okay, so if Walmart is aiming to set up edge computing for use by self-driving cars, there's a case to be made that any of those other firms might want to do likewise.

Maybe we'll end-up in an edge computing arms race, each firm putting up prized edge computers and trying to outdo the other.

One might advertise that they have faster processors, while another might say that their edge computers have a higher uptime factor.

Your self-driving car might get a discounted price on edge computing cycles for every Happy Meal that is sold while a passenger is inside that brand of driverless car, or your driverless car might get a free chocolate chip cookie for riders whenever the AI accesses a local Subway provided edge computer.

Endless possibilities.

The companies that make computers for edge computing have got to be salivating.

That being said, perhaps a dose of reality might be handy to add to this grandiose elixir.

Here's the rub.

If the basis for having the edge computing is to parlay into the real-time driving act of true self-driving cars, it's a recipe for disaster and a dog that won't hunt.

Sorry to crush those dreams.

But, before you get too dejected, we don't necessarily need to toss this baby out with the bathwater (ugh, not the most endearing metaphor), since there is a way to potentially salvage the overall concept.

I'll explain next why the foundational assumption is regrettably off base, and then offer some ways that the idea could be revised into being more practical.

Let's unpack the matter.

The Levels Of Self-Driving Cars

It is important to clarify what I mean when referring to self-driving cars.

True self-driving cars are ones that the AI drives the car entirely on its own and there isn't any human assistance during the driving task.

These driverless vehicles are considered a Level 4 and Level 5, while a car that requires a human driver to co-share the driving effort is usually considered at a Level 2 or Level 3. The cars that co-share the driving task are described as being semi-autonomous, and typically contain a variety of automated add-on's that are referred to as ADAS (Advanced Driver-Assistance Systems).

There is not yet a true self-driving car at Level 5, which we don't yet even know if this will be possible to achieve, and nor how long it will take to get there.

Meanwhile, the Level 4 efforts are gradually trying to get some traction by undergoing very narrow and selective public roadway trials, though there is controversy over whether this testing should be allowed per se (we are all life-or-death guinea pigs in an experiment taking place on our highways and byways, some point out).

Since semi-autonomous cars require a human driver, the adoption of those types of cars won't be markedly different than driving conventional vehicles, so there's not much to discuss related to this edge computing aspect (I'm not saying that semi-autonomous couldn't make use of such edge computers, and only suggesting that the need is less valued).

For semi-autonomous cars, it is important that you know about a disturbing aspect that's been arising lately, namely that in spite of those human drivers that keep posting videos of themselves falling asleep at the wheel of a Level 2 or Level 3 car, we all need to avoid being misled into believing that the driver can take away their attention from the driving task while driving a semi-autonomous car.

You are the responsible party for the driving actions of the vehicle, regardless of how much automation might be tossed into a Level 2 or Level 3.

Self-Driving Cars And External Reliance

For Level 4 and Level 5 true self-driving vehicles, there won't be a human driver involved in the driving task.

All occupants will be passengers.

The AI is doing the driving.

We are now at the juncture of popping the balloon on the idea of using edge computers during the act of driving a car for purposes of performing the driving task.

In brief, a true self-driving car is autonomous, meaning that it shouldn't need any outside assistance to drive the vehicle, and in fact, it "must not" have such a reliance per se.

Here's why.

Suppose the onboard AI is driving the car and relying upon an external edge computer to do so, perhaps an edge computer sitting in a local retail store.

All of a sudden, the electronic connection between the in-motion self-driving car gets disrupted, which can readily and easily occur for any number of reasons, and the AI can no longer communicate with the edge device.

What happens to the self-driving car, zipping along on the highway at say 65 miles per hour, as it is now presumably an unguided missile and lacks a connection to the nearby edge computer?

Would you feel safe inside that self-driving car, knowing that it has a dependence upon being able to drive the vehicle and can only do so with a guaranteed always-available remote connection?

I don't think so.

A few seconds of disconnection could lead to a disastrous car crash, and even split seconds could produce similarly untoward outcomes.

It's a very bad idea.

As I've elaborated in prior pieces, wireless cannot and must not be a safety-related use case for self-driving cars.

Furthermore, I cast doubt too on the idea of using remote human drivers, a concept perhaps similar to the notion of using edge computers, namely that this creates a highly dangerous dependence on something or someone outside of the car to make sure that the car drives properly and safely.

Some might argue that if a self-driving car is kept to slow speeds and if it has a fail-safe action of immediately stopping the vehicle, these kinds of remote dependencies are okay. Yes, in some limited circumstances that might be feasible, but it nonetheless is opening a can of worms.

Others argue that if we cannot create AI that can fully drive a car, we might have no choice but to allow for remote human drivers.

Well, there's a lot there to unpack, and let's just say that the AI ought not to be considered autonomous if it cannot drive the car on its own, and therefore this puts that type of car back into the semi-autonomous realm.

I typically liken this type of discussion to how humans drive.

By-and-large, I believe we can agree that the human driver of a car is the captain of the ship. They are responsible for driving the car. They don't require someone else that's remote to aid them in the actual driving of the car.
The moment-to-moment actions of driving the car are performed by that human driver.

Imagine if a human driver needed to be on the phone with someone else in order to know when and how to apply the brakes or hit the gas, along with also being reliant upon when and in what direction to steer the car.

As a passenger in such a situation, you would rightfully be mortified that if the cell phone connection drops, or if the phone itself malfunctions, you'll end up with a driver that is apparently unable to drive the car, and yet you are sitting there and completely powerless to do anything other than pray and hope that the phone connection gets reacquired.

If self-driving cars get pushed into the marketplace with a reliance on edge computers for undertaking the driving act, it will be a sad day for all.

There will undeniably be car accidents involving those kinds of self-driving cars and the public and regulators will come down on the suppression of further driverless car rollouts in a heartbeat.

Properly so.

More Ways To Go

You might recall that I alluded to the possibility that there might be more ways to skin this cat (oops, probably as coarse as saying the earlier bathwater remark).

Return to the analogy about human drivers.

A human driver might call a friend to get local directions about how to get to their house.

Notice that doing so does not intertwine with the moment-to-moment driving act, in the sense that the human driver is still fully able to drive the car, and they are merely getting some helpful directions from their friend.

The human driver is still able to navigate the streets on their own and avoid pesky jaywalking pedestrians, and otherwise, fully perform the driving task *on their own*.

A true self-driving car should be able to do likewise, meaning that it can fully drive the car, and if it uses any kind of external connection or remote driver it is doing so only as a supplement that is utilized above-and-beyond the driving act per se.

This takes us back to the use of edge computing.

It could be that the on-board AI might seek some supplemental analysis of collected sensory data, not because the AI cannot drive the car, and instead due to the possibility that the additional analyses might lead to finding say a more efficient path to take.

The on-board computer processors might already be consumed with the driving act, and thus the AI system opts to make a connection to a nearby edge computer and pump some data over to it, and then have the edge computer do a quick computational analysis, providing the results back to the onboard AI.

Keep in mind that if the edge computing connection drops during this process, it won't have any substantive impact on the AI and the driving of the self-driving car.

Sure, maybe the AI takes a longer path to the destination because it didn't get the more efficient path that might have been found via the edge computer, but nonetheless, the self-driving car is still driving safely and was not driving in a manner that was dependent on the edge computer.

In short, we can keep the edge computers in the picture and resurrect the idea of using them, opting to use those edge computers in these ways:

- For any non-safety related task that augments or supplements the onboard AI and yet does not pertain to the core driving act.

- For any safety-related task that isn't time-critical, and for which supplements the on-board AI, as though it was akin to having access to a useful second opinion, but again does not dovetail into the driving act itself.

- For purposes of being a store-and-forward processing point (I'll be covering this topic in a future column).

- Other possibilities as long as they aren't integral to the moment-to-moment driving task of the onboard AI.

Conclusion

Should retailers jump into this kind of mash-up?

Doubters would be quick to point out that having a retailer become an edge computing provider seems afield of their presumed core competencies of being a retailer.

Concerns include:

- Do they have the needed expertise to put in place the requisite edge computing devices and electronic networking and communications capabilities?

- Will they be able to maintain and support those capabilities over time?

- Are they prepared to cope with the lightning-fast pace of new tech that arises and therefore replace their edge computers on a timely and frequent enough cycle?

- They'll need to likely do all the same things that cloud providers do, including offering software for using the edge computers, troubleshooting the edge devices, and so on – do they realize the magnitude of this?

- Plus, this all needs to be done in a reliable, consistent manner and will necessitate those edge computers having the same high bar of uptime as would be found with a bona fide cloud service; thus, do they realize this isn't an easy picnic?

It's a bit of a tall order and certainly seems outside of the sphere that they normally operate in.

The other side of the coin is that if you believe that we are going to have a tremendous growth in the need for edge computing, maybe retailers ought to make sure they are part of that trend.

There are certainly other potential uses for those edge computers, and they don't need to only use them for self-driving car purposes.

Indeed, whether self-driving cars is a viable avenue is not even a necessity, and for the moment might simply be on the drawing board as future potential.

Taking a macroscopic perspective, let's tackle the self-driving car aspect on its own merits.

We already know that retailers are inevitably going to be involved with self-driving cars, one way or another:

- People that come to shop are going to use self-driving cars to get to the retailer.

- People that order goods online are going to have self-driving cars that bring those products to them from the retailer.

- Self-driving cars and self-driving trucks are going to be essential to any coming and going related activities for their brick-and-mortar locations.

Overall, retailers would be unwise and get caught behind the eight ball if they fail to do something related to self-driving cars.

Best sooner rather than later.

Inevitably, their core business is going to be highly dependent upon driverless cars.

It's going to be rough for them if others end-up controlling the means of getting customers to their stores and getting their products to their customers. Retailers will be forced into making deals with self-driving car owners, perhaps large firms owning fleets, and be at a disadvantage in those negotiations if they've not already themselves entered into the driverless realm.

I think you can see why then that retailers might be seriously pondering what to do about self-driving cars, along with contemplating what to do about edge computers.

There is perhaps a suitable place in that mash-up for retailers, but they need to be careful about which direction they go and not end up with a mishmash of a mash-up on their hands.

CHAPTER 9
STONEHENGE LESSONS
AND
AI SELF-DRIVING CARS

CHAPTER 9
STONEHENGE LESSONS
AND AI SELF-DRIVING CARS

Can something quite ancient provide insights for something modern and futuristic?

Well, we know that those that don't pay attention to history are oft to repeat it, so perhaps there is value in considering notable historical events and artifacts.

Stonehenge.

The word conjures up the iconic image of those large-sized stones that sit in a circular pattern and about which there is much intrigue and debate.

Residing in Wiltshire on the southern part of England, the hundred or so heavy and unwieldy stones attract nearly 1 million visitors each year.

Besides being a spectacle for the everyday person, the collected stones have been probed, scrutinized and analyzed by the likes of historians, architects, geologists, engineers, astronomers, philosophers, scientists, and a myriad of other experts.

Why is there such intense and enduring interest?

The inquiry stems from the aspect that these huge stones seemed to have been put in place around 5,000 years ago, during the Neolithic era, and perhaps came to gradually be moved into place over a period of 1,500 years.

Furthermore, the stones were presumably brought to the existing location from relatively far distances, meaning that somehow those hefty stones had to be moved to the present-day location (some of the stones weigh an astounding 40 tons and tower at a height of 24 feet tall).

How would people of that time period have possibly been able to move such weighty stones?

They didn't have the combustion engine, there weren't any tractors, and nor any kind of seemingly viable mechanical means of transportation at that time to lift or drag something so heavy and bulky.

Notably, estimates are that the wheel itself wasn't invented until about 3,500 B.C.

Experts further point out that the stones were presumably moved at a time that predated the construction of the pyramids, suggesting that it was unlikely that the sophisticated construction techniques invented for the pyramids was yet unknown.

Theories abound about what the moving process might have been.

Perhaps the heavy stones were floated on the sea and towed to Wiltshire, though it is useful to recognize that the location is landlocked, suggesting that one way or another there still had to be some amount of land-based traversal involved.

Did shifting glaciers by happenstance bring those stones close to the location and the people then managed to somehow manhandle the stones over the remaining land journey required?

Perhaps logs were used to essentially roll the heavy stones and get them to their desired spot?

Additionally, once the stones were miraculously gotten to the locale, some of the stones are set up in a crown or arch-like manner known as a trilithon.

Imagine that you had these massive stones and wanted to put them up in trilithon shape and had no kind of heavy lifting capabilities.

How could you do this?

Nobody knows for sure how they moved the stones to the location, and nobody knows for sure how they perched them up.

Of course, amidst the speculation comes the outside-of-the-box thinking that maybe some extraordinary means spirited the stones into their location and placement.

For example, some believe that sorcery was used.

Well, maybe.

Or, aliens from another planet provided a helping hand, or appendage, or whatever they might use to move big stones (possibly forcefield ray guns, or via the use of *the force* itself?).

Mark that into the category of UFO's and is presumably fully explained in Area 51.

For the moment, let's set aside how the stones came to be moved to the now revered spot, and ask an equally vital question: Why did people want those stones there and why were the stones placed into a circular formation?

Assuming that it would have taken a rather herculean effort to move the stones to the locale, consuming possibly hundreds or thousands of people and working persistently over hundreds or thousands of years, we would have to believe that there was a darned good reason for this mighty struggle.

On a survival basis, the act doesn't seem to pencil out.

Presumably, you would be best advised to consume your limited energies toward growing crops and hunting for food, a necessity for existence, or making a fortress to protect yourselves, rather than moving a bunch of really big rocks into a circle.

What good does it do to have those stones in that specific spot and arranged in that specific way?

Nobody knows.

Theories abound about the rationale involved.

It's a burial site, some say.

It was a religious holy place, some suggest.

Perhaps it was a place of healing.

Some of the rocks are a special type known as ringing rocks, possibly providing a clue about why those specific stones were used. The people of that era might have thought such stones had special powers for healing or for meditation or for other magical purposes.

Another theory is that the stones are a type of device, serving as an astronomical calendar.

The stones are arrayed in a manner to coincide with the winter solstice and the summer solstice.

This arrangement especially attracts visitors today during the solstices, believing that it's a remarkable place to be, including that it connects us to the past and to the grandness of nature.

Yet another theory is that the stones were put there in homage to the elites and leaders of that time period.

Perhaps it is a memorial to honor the rich and famous.

Generally, the whole topic is rife with mystery and intrigue.

Experts of all kinds have made attempts to explain what it is, how it came to be, why it was done, and so on.

The everyday person can choose to embrace one or more of those theories, or make-up their own theory instead.

Does any of this provide a historical context with possibly hidden lessons that could be surfaced and leveraged toward today's modern world?

Sure, why not.

Here's the question to ponder: *Does Stonehenge offer insights that can be used to further advance the advent of true self-driving cars?*

Yes, those ringing rocks have something to say.

Let's unpack the matter.

The Levels Of Self-Driving Cars

It is important to clarify what I mean when referring to true self-driving cars.

True self-driving cars are ones that the AI drives the car entirely on its own and there isn't any human assistance during the driving task.

These driverless vehicles are considered a Level 4 and Level 5, while a car that requires a human driver to co-share the driving effort is usually considered at a Level 2 or Level 3. The cars that co-share the driving task are described as being semi-autonomous, and typically contain a variety of automated add-on's that are referred to as ADAS (Advanced Driver-Assistance Systems).

There is not yet a true self-driving car at Level 5, which we don't yet even know if this will be possible to achieve, and nor how long it will take to get there.

Meanwhile, the Level 4 efforts are gradually trying to get some traction by undergoing very narrow and selective public roadway trials, though there is controversy over whether this testing should be allowed per se (we are all life-or-death guinea pigs in an experiment taking place on our highways and byways, some point out).

Since semi-autonomous cars require a human driver, the adoption of those types of cars won't be markedly different than driving conventional vehicles, so there's not much new per se to cover about them on this topic (though, as you'll see in a moment, the points next made are generally applicable).

For semi-autonomous cars, it is important that kids are forewarned about a disturbing aspect that's been arising lately, namely that in spite of those human drivers that keep posting videos of themselves falling asleep at the wheel of a Level 2 or Level 3 car, we all need to avoid being misled into believing that the driver can take away their attention from the driving task while driving a semi-autonomous car.

You are the responsible party for the driving actions of the vehicle, regardless of how much automation might be tossed into a Level 2 or Level 3.

Self-Driving Cars And Realistic Expectations

For Level 4 and Level 5 true self-driving vehicles, there won't be a human driver involved in the driving task.

All occupants will be passengers.

The AI is doing the driving.

What lessons are there from Stonehenge that could possibly apply to the most modern of technology?

Allow me to humbly offer the following applicable Stonehenge-based insights:

- **Intentions Not Self-Evident**

For Stonehenge, you cannot divine by inspection alone the basis for why the stones are there and what they are intending to convey or do.

It is not self-evident.

One of the criticisms being leveled at true self-driving cars is that the driving act of the AI might not be self-evident to humans that are nearby to the driverless car.

As a pedestrian, you today try to look in the eye of the human driver of a car coming down the street at you, attempting to gauge the intent of the driver.

Will the driver slow down or will they continue at their existing pace?

Will the driver let me cross the street or are they determined to go first and not let me cross?

Likewise, human drivers in cars nearby to a driverless car are often at odds about what the driverless car is going to do.

You can generally look at a human driver in another car and guess what the driver might do, such as cutting into your lane or trying to outpace you.

There isn't anyone seated in a driver's seat of a true self-driving car and therefore nobody that you can look at to gauge what the AI system is intending to do.

That's a problem.

There are solutions being pursued, including mounting on the exterior of self-driving cars an LED screen that displays the upcoming actions of the AI driving system. Some of these are perfunctory in their look-and-feel, others are using a catchy (maybe too cute) use of eyeball-like screens.

Anyway, when intentions are not self-evident, such as for Stonehenge and for AI driving systems, it can leave us all in a lurch.

- **It Must Be Sorcery Or Magic**

For Stonehenge, since we don't know for sure what or why it exists, some have resorted to suggesting that it came to be via the use of sorcery or magic.

In the case of true self-driving cars, some are so shocked to see a car driving itself that they mentally go off-the-rails and think that the AI is sentient or otherwise other-worldly.

This belief that the AI has extraordinary capabilities is problematic because it can mislead people into assuming that the AI driving system can do things that it cannot do.

For example, some keep saying that the AI will ensure that we never have any car-related deaths and nor car-related injuries ever again.

Nonsense.

A car is still a car.

A self-driving car is still a car.

If a child darts into the street without any in-advance warning and a self-driving car is coming down the street, the physics belies the chances of being able to stop in time or maneuver to avoid hitting the child. In short, we are still going to have some amount of car-related deaths and injuries, though hopefully a lot less than we have today.

Given the recent glorification of AI, some worry that people will fall victim to the false belief that AI is somehow all-knowing and all-seeing, implying that it cannot make mistakes and that it is perfect in comparison to human driving.

This is a myth.

• Lack Of An Explanation

For Stonehenge, there isn't any originating documentation to explain the origins and basis for the stones being there and what we ought to do about the stones.

Maybe if we had been provided with a kind of owner's manual, we might know today what the people of long ago had in mind.

You could even make the case that perhaps there is a means of leveraging Stonehenge now to our societal advantage in a modern era, yet we don't know what that might be.

So far, it pretty much sits there as a tourist attraction and otherwise doesn't add much value to our existing way of life (though the spark to our curiosity possibly provides some redeemable value and inexorably will reveal more lessons about the past).

One expressed concern about self-driving cars is a lack of explanatory capability to-date, and similarly, the same qualm is leveled at AI systems in general.

Here's what that means.

Some of the advances in AI lately have been due to the use of large-scale artificial neural networks, often also referred to as deep learning. These are nothing more than mathematical representations of simplistic arithmetic "neuron" computer-based simulations and are not anything on the scale and immensity of human neurons and human thinking.

Essentially, the AI neural networks are computational pattern matchers.

As these get bigger and more convoluted, we are increasingly losing the aspect of why the computational pattern matcher has ascertained a particular result. It is hopelessly enmeshed in a numerical web that lacks any kind of logically apparent explanation.

With humans, you can usually obtain a reasoning or explanation for their actions.

I ate the apple because I was hungry.

I opted to take a right at the light because the street ahead is busy with construction and it would be faster to make a right and go up to the next street to avoid the traffic snarl where the construction is taking place.

Right now, few of the automakers and self-driving tech firms are doing much to provide what's called XAI, or explainable AI.

Presumably, as a human passenger, you would normally be able to interact with a ridesharing driver, a human driver, and ask them to explain what they are doing.

Why did you make the right turn just now?

Is there some reason that we are driving so slowly?

People are inevitably going to want the AI of self-driving cars to be able to explain themselves.

Advances in Natural Language Processing (NLP) are already evident via our day-to-day use of systems such as Siri and Alexa.

Our expectation will be that if we are using AI driving systems to drive us around in driverless cars, by gosh, the AI ought to be able to explain what it is doing.

AI developers and self-driving tech makers that simply shrug their shoulders and say that we should blindly trust the mathematically derived models are going to discover that people won't relish a world of prevalent self-driving cars that aren't able to indicate the what and why of their driving efforts.

Currently, it is exciting to ride in a self-driving car and the few that are doing so aren't yet clamoring for XAI in the driving system, but once there are more driverless cars on our streets and more people riding in them, you can mark my words that explanatory AI driving systems will become a pressing need.

I doubt that we'll ever be able to get those massive stones at Stonehenge to talk with us, while in the case of today's AI and the future AI systems to come, we certainly should expect and insist that explanations go with the territory.

Conclusion

I trust that the use of Stonehenge as a living past that can be related to the present and future provided a bit of whimsy and thought rendering.

Could we put the shoe on the other foot?

In essence, maybe there's a means to have true self-driving cars provide lessons that would help unlock the mysteries of Stonehenge.

Or, in lieu of trying to consider how self-driving cars could apply, maybe we can craft an AI system that's devoted to cracking the secrets of Stonehenge.

Just as soon as I'm done getting my AI self-driving car to work, I'll switch over to the Stonehenge project and let you know what the AI hacking discovers.

CHAPTER 10

LEVELS OF AUTONOMY FEUD

AND

AI SELF-DRIVING CARS

CHAPTER 10

LEVELS OF AUTONOMY FEUD

AND

AI SELF-DRIVING CARS

Quick, how many senses do humans have?

Most of us would rattle off the five senses of hearing, seeing, tasting, touching, and the sense of being able to smell.

Everybody knows that.

So, your answer presumably is five.

There are some though that claim we have a sixth sense, perhaps consisting of intuition or an ability to have premonitions.

Okay, the answer is apparently six.

Actually, maybe there are seven senses since some assert that we have a sense of space, meaning that you are able to feel where your body resides within your space or area of movement, a sense often referred to as proprioception.

Which is it, do we have five senses, or six senses, or seven senses, or are there even more senses and could we have nine or ten of them?

The debate continues to rage on about the number of senses that humans have and right now there's no final answer, though the commonly accepted belief is that we have five senses.

There is a similar type of debate in the self-driving car industry regarding how many levels of autonomy can be best delineated.

Currently, the existing standard that is accepted by-and-large by self-driving car pros is that there are six levels of autonomy, which have been defined and promulgated by the Society of Automotive Engineers (SAE) and in conjunction with numerous other standards bodies.

The SAE standard indicates that these are the six levels of driving autonomy:
- Level 0: No Automation
- Level 1: Driver Automation
- Level 2: Partial Automation
- Level 3: Conditional Automation
- Level 4: High Automation
- Level 5: Full Automation

Notice that the levels are numbered from 0 to 5 (be careful interpreting the wording that is associated with each level, since those short phrases do not necessarily well encapsulate the full embodiment of each level as strictly defined by the standard).

Some don't like the aspect that the levels start with the number 0, since it becomes awkward to readily indicate how many levels there are. The topmost level is numbered 5, and thus some people mistakenly believe there are only five levels of autonomy.

If the numbering began with the number 1, you'd have levels 1, 2, 3, 4, 5, 6, and this would then be a more immediate tell that there are six levels of autonomy.

The counterargument is that the first of the several levels consists of no autonomy, therefore it deserves being considered simply as a level of zero.

If you were to give it the number of one as its level, the argument goes it would imply that there is some non-zero amount of autonomy included.

Plus, of course, computer people love to start things with the number 0, which though this doesn't often sit well with the general populace, as they say when you have the power of the pen you are able to write the rules.

Another occasional flare-up is that the numbers should be abandoned and letters ought to be used instead, suggesting that the levels would be the letters of the alphabet, presumably the letters a, b, c, d, e, f, though this has not caught any attention and pretty much is dead in the water.

Anyway, for the moment, put aside the acrimonious mudslinging about whether the levels should continue to be counted from 0 to 5 or be something else such as 1 to 6 or possibly a set of letters in the alphabet.

The key here is that just about everybody agrees that there are six levels of autonomy and somewhat amicably go along with the SAE standard accordingly.

Aha, there is always room for contention.

Not everyone does believe that there are just six levels of autonomy for driverless cars.

Some believe that there are more levels, including some pining away for 7 levels, some want 8 levels, and others have tried to get us to 9 or 10 levels.

If you are wondering whether anyone wants to reduce to say 5 levels, it's a rare argument, though going back to the 0 to 5 numbering there are those that say you shouldn't count the 0 level and therefore they assert that there are really only 5 legitimate levels.

Really?

Let's move on.

When I say that some are arguing for making the standard be more than 6 levels, I'd like to exclude those that generate and fabricate fake news about self-driving cars and have no idea what they are talking about.

In other words, the media regrettably at times will state that there are some umpteen numbers of levels and do so with ignorance about the SAE standard. There are some that don't know much about self-driving cars and will utter whatever seems to come to their minds.

We'll put aside the suggestions about being more than 6 levels that are proffered by those that aren't in the know, and for whom only say such things from the side of illiteracy or by the wanton act of wanting to seem controversial or outlandish.

Stick with the serious cases of wanting to expand the number of levels and please toss into the junk heap the foolhardy ones.

Why bring this topic up at all?

Because Honda has offered a teaser for their upcoming reveal at the tech haven CES (Consumer Electronics Show) in Las Vegas about a new self-driving concept car that they say showcases eight levels of autonomy.

Yes, read that again, they are going with 8 levels of autonomy, rather than the SAE standard and widely accepted and usually agreed with 6 levels of autonomy.

This has rankled some in the self-driving car industry.

You might be thinking that it is a tempest in a teapot and it doesn't matter how many levels of autonomy one wishes to define.

Oh, but you'd be missing the bigger picture if you believed that.

There are quite serious and important reasons to not be willy-nilly about the numbers of levels of autonomy.

Let's unpack the matter.

The Levels Of Self-Driving Cars

It is important to clarify what I mean when referring to self-driving cars.

True self-driving cars are ones that the AI drives the car entirely on its own and there isn't any human assistance during the driving task.

These driverless vehicles are considered a Level 4 and Level 5, while a car that requires a human driver to co-share the driving effort is usually considered at a Level 2 or Level 3. The cars that co-share the driving task are described as being semi-autonomous, and typically contain a variety of automated add-on's that are referred to as ADAS (Advanced Driver-Assistance Systems).

There is not yet a true self-driving car at Level 5, which we don't yet even know if this will be possible to achieve, and nor how long it will take to get there.

Meanwhile, the Level 4 efforts are gradually trying to get some traction by undergoing very narrow and selective public roadway trials, though there is controversy over whether this testing should be allowed per se (we are all life-or-death guinea pigs in an experiment taking place on our highways and byways, some point out).

For Level 4 and Level 5 true self-driving vehicles, there won't be a human driver involved in the driving task. All occupants will be passengers. The AI is doing the driving.

For semi-autonomous cars, it is important that people be forewarned about a disturbing aspect that's been arising lately, namely that in spite of those human drivers that keep posting videos of themselves falling asleep at the wheel of a Level 2 or Level 3 car, we all need to avoid being misled into believing that the driver can take away their attention from the driving task while driving a semi-autonomous car.

You are the responsible party for the driving actions of the vehicle, regardless of how much automation might be tossed into a Level 2 or Level 3.

Self-Driving Cars And Levels Debates

In the case of the Honda teaser, they have not yet stated what the 8 levels of autonomy consist of.

Guess we'll need to wait and see what they unveil at CES.

Is this then a clever marketing ploy to have floated the notion of eight levels and keep us all breathlessly awaiting the reveal?

Perhaps.

Though there is a downside to this approach.

For those that are already exasperated by the ongoing debate about the number of levels, they see this teaser as yet another attempt to make troubles where no such troubles ought to be.

It is, as the old saying goes, a needless poking of the eye of a bear.

Pros that have been down this trodden path too many times are apt to wearily ask: *Do we really need to revisit the levels of driverless autonomy again and again and again?*

Look, it's six levels, they cry out, and stop rattling the cage.

Worse too, if the eight levels are potentially untoward as reasonable suggestions, the concern is that we'll once again have the overall media pick-up on the topic and create more confusion among the public and regulators.

It could be that the eight levels are not especially useful or usable as a means of structuring the levels of driverless autonomy and sadly, regrettably, might foster confusion and angst.

We all know about the clutter of now-famous (or infamous) new marketing ploys that ended-up turning themselves upside down and inadvertently started a storm rather than calming the seas.

The law of unintended consequences.

Time will tell in this case.

Ways To Go Beyond Six By Splitting Hairs

Now we might nonetheless consider in what ways the six levels versus more levels issue even arises.

Where's the beef, you might be asking.

One of the most common ways to go beyond the existing six levels of self-driving autonomy consists of seeking to blowout the existing levels.

Here's what that means.

For Level 2, which many would suggest that Tesla's with AutoPilot are currently at, some try to say that the Tesla is really at a level of 2.5, meaning that they acknowledge it is not yet at level 3, but they also argue that it is much more than merely level 2 in terms of being at the floor of level 2.

As such, this same kind of logic has been used for the other levels too.

Some believe that there should be a level 2, 2.5, 3, 3.5, 4, 4.5, 5, 5.5.

Note that this would add four additional levels (shown as 2.5, 3.5, 4.5, 5.5), assuming that you were willing to call the intermediary stages as levels (which some argue you would not do).

If you added those four to the existing six, you'd have a grand total of ten levels.

There is controversy about this, including the aspect that if you are going to have a level 5.5, shouldn't you also have a level of 6 (adding even one more level to the pile and making it into 11 levels)?

This argument about having intermediary levels was seemingly already settled due to the aspect that the SAE standard clearly states that there is no such thing as an intermediary level.

If you have automation that fulfills a level, the car is then ranked or scored as being at that level.

If the automation does not fulfill a level, it is not considered as ranked or scored at that level.

Case closed.

Well, despite the stated rules, there are still some that argue we need to have intermediary states in the autonomy structure.

Those making such an argument then fall into one of two camps, namely you can refer to the intermediary states as sublevels and not count them as honest-to-goodness levels, or you ought to count them as full-fledged levels (in which case, perhaps renumber all of the levels and make it into the numbers of 0 to 10, or 1 to 11, or however you want).

Some would say that doing so is merely rearranging the chairs on the deck of the ocean liner.

Sure, it might be helpful to have those sublevels clearly identified, and it might then be easier for automakers and self-driving tech firms to assert more definitively what level of automation they are providing in their car.

But, it is an argument that some say opens a can of worms.

If we allow for those intermediary states, it could be a snowball that beings to roll down the hill.

After having available say a 2.5, someone might come along and insist we should have a 2.7 too. Someone else clamors for a 2.9. And so on.

Once you begin to splinter the levels, it could become a never-ending game.

Don't do it, we are warned since this splitting of hairs will become unwieldy, be impossible to well communicate to the public and regulators and make a mockery of the autonomy scheme.

Tantamount to hair-splitting, one might chortle.

Expanding The Levels For New Stuff

Step away from the sublevel splitting aspects.

Is there anything that might be missing from the existing levels and for which a case could be made to expand the number of levels?

Some say yes, there is such a case.

First, keep in mind that the existing SAE standard states that it applies only to on-road driving.

That makes sense in that most of the time we are driving our cars on streets and roads.

Of course, people do go off-road driving too.

Maybe there should be a level 6, consisting of autonomy for off-road driving, and thus expand the number of levels to seven (ranging from 0 to 6).

Secondly, the existing SAE standard refers to human driving as based on being able to drive a car in user manageable ways.

Some have criticized the lack of clear-cut meaning to what human driving consists of, since how I drive and how someone else drives could be quite different in terms of driving skill levels. A racetrack or Indy driver presumably knows a lot more about driving a car than you or I do.

Should driverless cars be held to being able to drive as could the best of human drivers, or be allowed to drive at the level of an average human driver (I've made the case that right now the aim is even lower, pretty much at the level of a teenage novice driver).

And, you could argue that we ultimately would want the AI to drive better than any human driver could, surpassing all human driving skills.

It seems like a laudable goal.

We might then add a level 7, which consists of autonomy that can drive a car better than any human proficiency, including better than the best of the best of racecar drivers.

That's now 8 levels of autonomy.

No clue as to whether that's the same as the Honda reveal or not.

One complaint about both the off-road addition and the mighty-driver notion is that rather than expanding the levels, we might be wiser to infuse those elements into the existing levels.

In essence, no need to toss out the six levels, and instead tweak and revise them to add whatever additional sauces we want to include.

You could readily argue that by infusing any new elements you will produce a more parsimonious result.

Maybe, or you might imprudently be trying to put eight pounds of rocks into a six-pound bag.

Conclusion

I've not yet fully explained why this all matters.

It's a big deal because we need to have an agreed to and in-common parlance to describe what the levels of autonomy are.

Suppose an automaker proudly proclaims that they have a self-driving car that has achieved level X, but there is no definitive meaning for what level X is. Meanwhile, another automaker claims their self-driving car is at a level of X+1, implying that their driverless car is better than the other automaker's self-driving car.

In the end, without a referee and some set of rules, it would be like playing a football game that hasn't established how many points you get for a touchdown.

Nobody would readily know what the score is and how each of the teams is doing.

Right now, we have an existing standard that's a generally accepted barometer, delineating six levels of autonomy for driverless cars, and it is a line-in-the-sand for automakers, self-driving tech firms, regulators, the public, and all other stakeholders that care about autonomous and semi-autonomous cars.

If anyone and especially those in authority opts to make-up additional levels or mess with the existing levels, doing so will certainly create consternation and produce many difficulties, especially if done in an arbitrary or capricious manner.

Pointedly, it's not that we should freeze in place the existing standard and never seek to change it, but instead, the notion that let's go ahead and consider ways to improve and upgrade the standard, working in concert with the appropriate standards bodies and associations.

That sure seems like a level-headed way to do things and I hope that we all do continue to find ways to tweak and revise the standard for the betterment of us all.

CHAPTER 11

HIDE AND ESCAPE

VIA

AI SELF-DRIVING CARS

CHAPTER 11

HIDE AND ESCAPE

VIA

AI SELF-DRIVING CARS

Recent news reports speculate that automotive titan Carlos Ghosn might have made his escape from Japan via hiding inside a large black case that would normally contain audio equipment used at a concert.

This kind of subterfuge seems reminiscent of the Cold War era and spy-versus-spy tactics.

Those of you that are movie buffs might recall the scene in *Torn Curtain* when Paul Newman and Julie Andrews are hiding inside a box that is being lifted off a boat that has just docked (I won't say what happens next, so no spoiler alert needed).

In any case, today's world is so chock full of video cameras that it is becoming increasingly difficult to affect a successful hide-and-escape scheme.

There are video surveillance cameras on rooftops, and on traffic signals, and on the sides of office buildings, and most pedestrians have their smartphone cameras at the ready to snap a pic or grab a video.

It seems if you can't get your five minutes of fame directly, you can at least capture something worthy of fame via your smartphone camera and then relish the afterglow of doing so.

Even our commonplace doorbells are now adorned with cameras, allowing video footage of anything happening in front of your home and taking place in the nearby street.

Part of the hide-and-escape modus operandi is that you oftentimes need to be spirited from point A to point B, most likely using a car.

Here's an interesting question: *Will the advent of true self-driving cars make it easier or harder to carry out a successful hide-and-escape ploy?*

Let's unpack the matter and see.

The Levels Of Self-Driving Cars

It is important to clarify what I mean when referring to true self-driving cars.

True self-driving cars are ones that the AI drives the car entirely on its own and there isn't any human assistance during the driving task.

These driverless vehicles are considered a Level 4 and Level 5, while a car that requires a human driver to co-share the driving effort is usually considered at a Level 2 or Level 3. The cars that co-share the driving task are described as being semi-autonomous, and typically contain a variety of automated add-on's that are referred to as ADAS (Advanced Driver-Assistance Systems).

There is not yet a true self-driving car at Level 5, which we don't yet even know if this will be possible to achieve, and nor how long it will take to get there.

Meanwhile, the Level 4 efforts are gradually trying to get some traction by undergoing very narrow and selective public roadway trials, though there is controversy over whether this testing should be allowed per se (we are all life-or-death guinea pigs in an experiment taking place on our highways and byways, some point out).

Since semi-autonomous cars require a human driver, the adoption of those types of cars won't be markedly different than driving conventional vehicles, so there's not much new per se to cover about them on this topic (though, as you'll see in a moment, the points next made are generally applicable).

For semi-autonomous cars, it is important that kids are forewarned about a disturbing aspect that's been arising lately, namely that in spite of those human drivers that keep posting videos of themselves falling asleep at the wheel of a Level 2 or Level 3 car, we all need to avoid being misled into believing that the driver can take away their attention from the driving task while driving a semi-autonomous car.

You are the responsible party for the driving actions of the vehicle, regardless of how much automation might be tossed into a Level 2 or Level 3.

Self-Driving Cars As An Aid To Hide-And-Escape

For Level 4 and Level 5 true self-driving vehicles, there won't be a human driver involved in the driving task.

All occupants will be passengers.

The AI is doing the driving.

Voila, the fact that the AI is doing the driving is a crucial element as to why a true self-driving car makes a handy hide-and-escape mechanism.

There isn't a human driver needed and therefore there isn't an eyewitness involved in the driving of the getaway car.

Neat!

Not only does this eliminate the eyewitness driver, the aspect that you are using the AI to drive also means that you don't need to try and find a human driver that's willing to be in on the secret.

It's kind of messy to have to bring a human driver into the fold of what is surreptitiously taking place. You might need to pay them extra dough, or worse still they might decide to spill the beans, and so on.

If you decide to use an ordinary driver that's not informed about the plot, you are at a constant risk that the driver might somehow suspect foul play is underway. The driver might then decide midstream to suddenly stop the car and run away.

Or, the driver might tattle the moment that the car journey has ended.

So, no human driver means no need to cope with an accomplice, either one overtly included or one that was a patsy.

That resolutely deals with the aspect of how the AI helps by taking the human driver out of the spy-versus-spy equation.

But, wait, there's more.

Would you need to be hidden inside a box, a crate, or some other container?

Not necessarily.

You could potentially enter directly into the self-driving car and then calmly exit when you've reached your destination.

Those of you that are budding spies might say that this leaves the person visible during the driving journey and that any commoner on the street might snag a photo of the person (presumably turning in the pic to TMZ), along with capturing the license plates, and the gig would be up.

Well, keep in mind that it is anticipated that the automakers might ultimately get rid of the conventional windows of a car.

This might be done to allow passengers to have complete seclusion inside a self-driving car, plus the inner walls of the car would have large LED displays.

These LED displays enable riders to watch streaming videos as they commute to work or carry on conversations via Facetime-like video interaction with their officemates. If you want to look outside, all you'll need to do is switch the video feed to the cameras that are already mounted on the self-driving car and you can watch the world around you.

The point is that no one can readily see who is in such a driverless car.

Perfect!

Suppose though that you only have available to you a self-driving car that hasn't yet switched over to replacing the windows with something non-transparent (or that can't yet be toggled from transparent to opaque)?

Wear a disguise.

Again, there's no human driver that can take a close-up look at you and potentially see the make-up and fake beard or wig that you are using.

Furthermore, once inside the self-driving car, you can simply lay down and for the rest of the ride be hidden from prying eyes outside of the driverless car.

In a conventional car with a human driver, you'd probably have a lot of explaining to do if you opted to lay down in the backseat. Maybe claim that you are feeling lightheaded or that your spleen has burst.

For the AI system, there's no need for you to explain a darned thing.

Just lay down.

And, another bonus about self-driving cars is that they are likely to be equipped to allow people to catch a nap or get some sleep.

The seats in self-driving cars will recline and enable passengers to rest while on their way to work or do so after a tough day at the office. When you reach your home, you'll feel refreshed and ready to interact with the family and your cherished pet dog and beloved cat.

Hiding inside a driverless car is going to be easy as pie.

All in all, you can expect that you'll either be inside a self-driving car that provides a feature to prevent being seen inside of the self-driving car, or you can readily laydown, cover yourself with a blanket, and zillions of other people will be doing the same in their self-driving cars too.

Nothing out of the ordinary in an era of true self-driving cars.

We need to add a bonus to the bonus.

If you still felt that there was a chance of being detected while inside the self-driving car, you could presumably ride in the trunk.

Yes, the trunk of the driverless car might be a possibility.

A human driver would certainly question why you are desirous of riding in the trunk. The story you'd need to tell would have to be quite fanciful, perhaps saying that you grew up in a family of contortionists and it relaxes you to be in a confined space.

The AI won't care.

You request a driverless car, it arrives, you open the trunk as though you are going to put your bags into it, and opt to crawl in.

Next, you instruct the AI to proceed, perhaps doing so on your smartphone and the driverless car heads on the driving journey.

You might be tempted to think that during the driving journey this would catch the eye of passerby that happens to see a driverless car going past them and the self-driving car is completely empty.

Actually, we are going to have lots of driverless cars roaming our streets and being empty a lot of the time.

The notion is that self-driving cars will be continually on the move, rather than being parked, and will be available at a moment's notice to any passenger that wants a lift. Indeed, I've decried the aspect that we might end up with a vast parade of empty driverless cars and this doesn't seem like a necessarily good thing for mankind (see **my link here**).

Also, realize that driverless cars are going to be used as delivery vehicles, taking goods from the local grocery to your house, and as such there will be numerous seemingly empty driverless cars on our highways and byways all of the time.

Okay, so you could ride inside a self-driving car and either be hidden from view or if somehow you are viewable you might wear a disguise and there's nobody else in the driverless car to rat you out.

Getting into the self-driving car is a potential point of being exposed, and likewise getting out of the self-driving car.

Think again about the AI aspects.

The AI won't have qualms about where you want to be picked-up and nor where you want to be dropped off (as an aside, the drop-off juncture is a difficult question still to be resolved since human drivers tend to use human judgment about the best spot to drop someone off, and the AI isn't yet at that capability).

In short, you can instruct the AI to pick you up at whatever location the driverless car can arrive at, and the same goes for the drop-off point.

Thus, you can arrange for a clandestine spot and the AI will abide by the request.

A human driver would likely start asking pesky questions.

No human driver, no prying questions.

It would seem that a true self-driving car is a godsend for those that might want to hide-and-escape.

Not entirely so.

Self-Driving Cars Defeating Hide-And-Escape

There are some hurdles to using a true self-driving car for your hide-and-escape plots.

First, assuming you don't own a self-driving car, you'll need to request one on a ridesharing basis.

Pundits are saying that self-driving cars will only be owned by large corporations and made available via a fleet for ridesharing purposes to the public.

I'm a bit of a contrarian in that I assert that we will still have individual ownership of cars, which logically makes sense since you'll likely be able to make money by owning a driverless car that you put out for ridesharing when you don't need to use it.

Anyway, let's assume for the moment that for your getaway car you are going to use one that is a ridesharing driverless car.

This means that you'll need to make a request to the ridesharing network and wait for a driverless car to show-up.

Depending upon whether the timing of your effort needs to be precise, you are now at the vagaries of the ridesharing service.

It might also be the case that you need to provide some form of identification when making the request, and thus need to have a false identity ready to be used.

Not to worry, though, since the odds are that the ridesharing networks won't especially care about identity and you can readily spoof it or find an easy way around it. Keep in mind that the ridesharing of driverless cars won't be like going to the airport and having to deal with the TSA.

So, don't sweat the identity aspects.

Unfortunately, there will be a record of the driverless car going from point A to point B, and this record might someday be used against you in a court of law or be used to ferret out where you are next residing.

Here's how that works.

For self-driving cars, they will be outfitted with OTA (Over-The-Air) electronic communications.

The OTA will be used to push software updates down into the AI of the driverless car by the automaker or self-driving tech firms. In addition, the self-driving car will pump-up to the cloud the data that's collected by the driverless car, such as the sensor data from the cameras, LIDAR, radar, and the like.

Thus, your AI self-driving car will be a bit of a tattletale.

Besides capturing a record of your journey, the odds are that driverless cars will have cameras pointed inward too.

The logic of having inward-pointing cameras is that the owners of the self-driving cars will want to make sure that riders don't trash the interior of the driverless car. By having a camera pointed at the passengers, this might prevent graffiti or at least capture video of those that do such a dastardly thing.

Furthermore, in general, you might purposely want an inward-facing camera so that you can carry on those Skype-like video interactions. When using such a feature to chat with your kids at home, they can see you as you wave at them and smile a reassurance that you'll certainly help them with their homework when you get home later that night.

Shucks, an inward-facing camera is nearly as bad as having a human driver as a witness.

Nope, not nearly so.

The odds are that some driverless car fleets will allow you to turn off the camera for privacy reasons.

The owner might offer this option to induce you to use their ridesharing driverless cars over their competition. Or, the owner could use this to charge added fees to turn off the camera, allowing the owner to remain competitive on the per-mile price of ridesharing driverless car use and yet still make some added clamshells.

In a worst-case scenario, you could simply cover the inward-facing cameras, and assuming that the system wasn't the wiser, away you go, scot-free.

Overall, these downsides aren't insurmountable hurdles.

The real rub involves the chances of getting nabbed while riding inside a driverless car.

Here's why.

With a human driver, you could potentially tell them to stomp on the gas, as needed, presumably to evade the police or otherwise avoid getting caught.

That's a no go for the AI.

Most are anticipating that the AI of driverless cars will be programmed to pretty much obey the law.

No speeding.

No wild maneuvers.

If somehow there is a possibility that someone wants to get you, and they know you are inside a self-driving car, you are essentially a sitting duck (for my concerns about carjackings, or known colloquially as robojackings of driverless cars).

Via OTA, it would be readily possible to find out from the AI the path of the driving journey that is taking place.

Cops would merely wait at the destination for you to arrive into their waiting hands.

Sweet!

Or, should I say, foiled.

Plus, via the OTA, the driving destination could be altered and take you directly to the police station.

Just in case you might figure out that your ride is being diverted, another possibility would be to have the police meet you along your driving journey. You'd have no apparent way to know that the police were using the OTA and the AI to monitor your driving progress and had found a convenient spot to then rendezvous and arrest you.

There is the possibility too that the police could instruct the self-driving car to come to a halt if perchance they came upon the driverless car while say on the freeway and suspected that you were hiding inside of it (see **the link here** about ways to stop a self-driving car).

The biggest loophole in the driverless car scheme for hide-and-escape will be that if you are found out or someone tells about your self-driving car journey, you've lost the ability to use the car as a getaway vehicle that would use screeching tires and tricky maneuvers to get away from the long arm of the law.

Bonnie and Clyde would not have welcomed true self-driving cars.

Conclusion

Some might be disturbed at this discussion about using driverless cars for undertaking a hide-and-escape jaunt.

Won't this let crooks know what to do?

Let's not be naïve and think that crooks aren't going to find ways to try and leverage self-driving cars to their own advantage (for how criminals might use self-driving cars to commit crimes).

For those that are willing to simply toss driverless cars into our society and not anticipate the good and foul ways that they will be used, it's a timeworn approach to bringing new innovations into our culture and by now we ought to be a bit more sophisticated.

Better to anticipate what might occur, even adversely, and prepare for it, rather than take a head-in-the-sand mindset and pretend we are living in a Utopian world.

There are a multitude of ways that the automakers and self-driving tech firms can craft the AI systems to reduce or mitigate criminal acts that might attempt to employ driverless cars, though such anti-crime mechanisms are not necessarily on the priority list since right now the goal is to achieve the already moonshot-like stretch goal of simply having self-driving cars that can take people on everyday driving journeys, doing so safely.

One inherent aspect of the existing approach to the AI driving systems is that there's little chance of a John Dillinger like means of evading federal agents and driving frenetically away from a crime scene.

Instead, it will be akin to having a driver that wants to come to a full stop at stop signs, won't run any red lights, and will make sure to stay just under the posted speed limit.

It's enough to make a grown mobster cry.

Lance B. Eliot

APPENDIX

APPENDIX A
TEACHING WITH THIS MATERIAL

The material in this book can be readily used either as a supplemental to other content for a class, or it can also be used as a core set of textbook material for a specialized class. Classes where this material is most likely used include any classes at the college or university level that want to augment the class by offering thought provoking and educational essays about AI and self-driving cars.

In particular, here are some aspects for class use:

o   Computer Science. Studying AI, autonomous vehicles, etc.

o   Business. Exploring technology and it adoption for business.

o   Sociology. Sociological views on the adoption and advancement of technology.

Specialized classes at the undergraduate and graduate level can also make use of this material.

For each chapter, consider whether you think the chapter provides material relevant to your course topic. There is plenty of opportunity to get the students thinking about the topic and force them to decide whether they agree or disagree with the points offered and positions taken. I would also encourage you to have the students do additional research beyond the chapter material presented (I provide next some suggested assignments they can do).

RESEARCH ASSIGNMENTS ON THESE TOPICS

Your students can find background material on these topics, doing so in various business and technical publications. I list below the top ranked AI related journals. For business publications, I would suggest the usual culprits such as the Harvard Business Review, Forbes, Fortune, WSJ, and the like.

Here are some suggestions of homework or projects that you could assign to students:

a) <u>Assignment for foundational AI research topic</u>: Research and prepare a paper and a presentation on a specific aspect of Deep AI, Machine Learning, ANN, etc. The paper should cite at least 3 reputable sources. Compare and contrast to what has been stated in this book.

b) <u>Assignment for the Self-Driving Car topic</u>: Research and prepare a paper and Self-Driving Cars. Cite at least 3 reputable sources and analyze the characterizations. Compare and contrast to what has been stated in this book.

c) <u>Assignment for a Business topic</u>: Research and prepare a paper and a presentation on businesses and advanced technology. What is hot, and what is not? Cite at least 3 reputable sources. Compare and contrast to the depictions in this book.

d) <u>Assignment to do a Startup:</u> Have the students prepare a paper about how they might startup a business in this realm. They must submit a sound Business Plan for the startup. They could also be asked to present their Business Plan and so should also have a presentation deck to coincide with it.

You can certainly adjust the aforementioned assignments to fit to your particular needs and the class structure. You'll notice that I ask for 3 reputable cited sources for the paper writing based assignments. I usually steer students toward "reputable" publications, since otherwise they will cite some oddball source that has no credentials other than that they happened to write something and post it onto the Internet. You can define "reputable" in whatever way you prefer, for example some faculty think Wikipedia is not reputable while others believe it is reputable and allow students to cite it.

The reason that I usually ask for at least 3 citations is that if the student only does one or two citations they usually settle on whatever they happened to find the fastest. By requiring three citations, it usually seems to force them to look around, explore, and end-up probably finding five or more, and then whittling it down to 3 that they will actually use.

I have not specified the length of their papers, and leave that to you to tell the students what you prefer. For each of those assignments, you could end-up with a short one to two pager, or you could do a dissertation length paper. Base the length on whatever best fits for your class, and the credit amount of the assignment within the context of the other grading metrics you'll be using for the class.

I mention in the assignments that they are to do a paper and prepare a presentation. I usually try to get students to present their work. This is a good practice for what they will do in the business world. Most of the time, they will be required to prepare an analysis and present it. If you don't have the class time or inclination to have the students present, then you can of course cut out the aspect of them putting together a presentation.

If you want to point students toward highly ranked journals in AI, here's a list of the top journals as reported by *various citation counts sources* (this list changes year to year):

- o   Communications of the ACM
- o   Artificial Intelligence
- o   Cognitive Science
- o   IEEE Transactions on Pattern Analysis and Machine Intelligence
- o   Foundations and Trends in Machine Learning
- o   Journal of Memory and Language
- o   Cognitive Psychology
- o   Neural Networks
- o   IEEE Transactions on Neural Networks and Learning Systems
- o   IEEE Intelligent Systems
- o   Knowledge-based Systems

GUIDE TO USING THE CHAPTERS

For each of the chapters, I provide next some various ways to use the chapter material. You can assign the tasks as individual homework assignments, or the tasks can be used with team projects for the class. You can easily layout a series of assignments, such as indicating that the students are to do item "a" below for say Chapter 1, then "b" for the next chapter of the book, and so on.

a) What is the main point of the chapter and describe in your own words the significance of the topic,

b) Identify at least two aspects in the chapter that you agree with, and support your concurrence by providing at least one other outside researched item as support; make sure to explain your basis for disagreeing with the aspects,

c) Identify at least two aspects in the chapter that you disagree with, and support your disagreement by providing at least one other outside researched item as support; make sure to explain your basis for disagreeing with the aspects,

d) Find an aspect that was not covered in the chapter, doing so by conducting outside research, and then explain how that aspect ties into the chapter and what significance it brings to the topic,

e) Interview a specialist in industry about the topic of the chapter, collect from them their thoughts and opinions, and readdress the chapter by citing your source and how they compared and contrasted to the material,

f) Interview a relevant academic professor or researcher in a college or university about the topic of the chapter, collect from them their thoughts and opinions, and readdress the chapter by citing your source and how they compared and contrasted to the material,

g) Try to update a chapter by finding out the latest on the topic, and ascertain whether the issue or topic has now been solved or whether it is still being addressed, explain what you come up with.

The above are all ways in which you can get the students of your class involved in considering the material of a given chapter. You could mix things up by having one of those above assignments per each week, covering the chapters over the course of the semester or quarter.

As a reminder, here are the chapters of the book and you can select whichever chapters you find most valued for your particular class:

Chapter Title

1   Eliot Framework for AI Self-Driving Cars

2   Your Bucket List and AI Self-Driving Cars

3   Highway Stunts and AI Self-Driving Cars

4   Future Wonderment and AI Self-Driving Cars

5   AI On-The-Fly Learning and AI Self-Driving Cars

6   Level 4 and Level 5 of AI Self-Driving Cars

7   Explaining Key Acronyms of AI Self-Driving Cars

8   Walmart Edge Computing and AI Self-Driving Cars

9   Stonehenge Lessons and AI Self-Driving Cars

10   Levels of Autonomy Feud and AI Self-Driving Cars

11   Hide and Escape Via AI Self-Driving Cars

Companion Book By This Author

Advances in AI and Autonomous Vehicles: Cybernetic Self-Driving Cars

Practical Advances in Artificial Intelligence (AI) and Machine Learning

by

Dr. Lance B. Eliot, MBA, PhD

This title is available via Amazon and other book sellers

Companion Book By This Author

Self-Driving Cars:
"The Mother of All AI Projects"

by Dr. Lance B. Eliot, MBA, PhD

This title is available via Amazon and other book sellers

This title is available via Amazon and other book sellers

This title is available via Amazon and other book sellers

Companion Book By This Author

Introduction to
Driverless Self-Driving Cars

by Dr. Lance B. Eliot, MBA, PhD

Chapter Title

This title is available via Amazon and other book sellers

This title is available via Amazon and other book sellers

<u>Companion Book By This Author</u>
Transformative Artificial Intelligence Driverless Self-Driving Cars
by Dr. Lance B. Eliot, MBA, PhD

<u>Chapter Title</u>

This title is available via Amazon and other book sellers

Companion Book By This Author

Disruptive Artificial Intelligence and Driverless Self-Driving Cars

by Dr. Lance B. Eliot, MBA, PhD

Chapter Title

This title is available via Amazon and other book sellers

Companion Book By This Author

State-of-the-Art
AI Driverless Self-Driving Cars

by Dr. Lance B. Eliot, MBA, PhD

Chapter Title

This title is available via Amazon and other book sellers

Companion Book By This Author

Top Trends in
AI Self-Driving Cars

by Dr. Lance B. Eliot, MBA, PhD

This title is available via Amazon and other book sellers

This title is available via Amazon and other book sellers

This title is available via Amazon and other book sellers

Companion Book By This Author

Sociotechnical Insights and AI Driverless Cars

by Dr. Lance B. Eliot, MBA, PhD

Chapter Title

1 Eliot Framework for AI Self-Driving Cars

2 Start-ups and AI Self-Driving Cars

3 Code Obfuscation and AI Self-Driving Cars

4 Hyperlanes and AI Self-Driving Cars

5 Passenger Panic Inside an AI Self-Driving Car

6 Tech Stockholm Syndrome and Self-Driving Cars

7 Paralysis and AI Self-Driving Cars

8 Ugly Zones and AI Self-Driving Cars

9 Ridesharing and AI Self-Driving Cars

10 Multi-Party Privacy and AI Self-Driving Cars

11 Chaff Bugs and AI Self-Driving Cars

12 Social Reciprocity and AI Self-Driving Cars

13 Pet Mode and AI Self-Driving Cars

This title is available via Amazon and other book sellers

Companion Book By This Author

Pioneering Advances for AI Driverless Cars

by Dr. Lance B. Eliot, MBA, PhD

Chapter Title

This title is available via Amazon and other book sellers

Companion Book By This Author

Leading Edge Trends for AI Driverless Cars

by Dr. Lance B. Eliot, MBA, PhD

This title is available via Amazon and other book sellers

Companion Book By This Author

The Cutting Edge of AI Autonomous Cars

by Dr. Lance B. Eliot, MBA, PhD

Chapter Title

This title is available via Amazon and other book sellers

Companion Book By This Author

The Next Wave of
AI Self-Driving Cars

by Dr. Lance B. Eliot, MBA, PhD

This title is available via Amazon and other book sellers

Companion Book By This Author

Revolutionary Innovations of AI Self-Driving Cars

by Dr. Lance B. Eliot, MBA, PhD

This title is available via Amazon and other book sellers

This title is available via Amazon and other book sellers

Companion Book By This Author

Trailblazing Trends for
AI Self-Driving Cars

by Dr. Lance B. Eliot, MBA, PhD

This title is available via Amazon and other book sellers

Companion Book By This Author

Ingenious Strides for
AI Driverless Cars

by Dr. Lance B. Eliot, MBA, PhD

This title is available via Amazon and other book sellers

Companion Book By This Author

AI Self-Driving Cars
Inventiveness

by Dr. Lance B. Eliot, MBA, PhD

This title is available via Amazon and other book sellers

This title is available via Amazon and other book sellers

Companion Book By This Author

Spearheading
AI Self-Driving Cars

by Dr. Lance B. Eliot, MBA, PhD

Chapter Title

This title is available via Amazon and other book sellers

<u>Companion Book By This Author</u>

Spurring
AI Self-Driving Cars

by Dr. Lance B. Eliot, MBA, PhD

<u>Chapter Title</u>

This title is available via Amazon and other book sellers

Companion Book By This Author

Avant-Garde
AI Driverless Cars

by Dr. Lance B. Eliot, MBA, PhD

Chapter Title

This title is available via Amazon and other book sellers

<u>Companion Book By This Author</u>

AI Self-Driving Cars
Evolvement

by Dr. Lance B. Eliot, MBA, PhD

<u>Chapter Title</u>

This title is available via Amazon and other book sellers

Companion Book By This Author

AI Driverless Cars
Chrysalis
by Dr. Lance B. Eliot, MBA, PhD

<u>Chapter Title</u>

This title is available via Amazon and other book sellers

Companion Book By This Author

Boosting
AI Autonomous Cars
by Dr. Lance B. Eliot, MBA, PhD

This title is available via Amazon and other book sellers

Companion Book By This Author

AI Self-Driving Cars
Trendsetting

by Dr. Lance B. Eliot, MBA, PhD

This title is available via Amazon and other book sellers

This title is available via Amazon and other book sellers

Companion Book By This Author

AI Autonomous Cars
Emergence

by Dr. Lance B. Eliot, MBA, PhD

This title is available via Amazon and other book sellers

Companion Book By This Author

AI Autonomous Cars Progress

by Dr. Lance B. Eliot, MBA, PhD

Chapter Title

This title is available via Amazon and other book sellers

Companion Book By This Author

AI Self-Driving Cars
Prognosis

by Dr. Lance B. Eliot, MBA, PhD

This title is available via Amazon and other book sellers

Lance B. Eliot

Companion Book By This Author

AI Self-Driving Cars
Momentum

by Dr. Lance B. Eliot, MBA, PhD

This title is available via Amazon and other book sellers

<u>Companion Book By This Author</u>

AI Self-Driving Cars
Headway

by Dr. Lance B. Eliot, MBA, PhD

<u>Chapter Title</u>

This title is available via Amazon and other book sellers

Lance B. Eliot

Companion Book By This Author

AI Self-Driving Cars
Vicissitude

by Dr. Lance B. Eliot, MBA, PhD

Chapter Title

This title is available via Amazon and other book sellers

Companion Book By This Author

AI Self-Driving Cars
Autonomy

by Dr. Lance B. Eliot, MBA, PhD

Chapter Title

This title is available via Amazon and other book sellers

ABOUT THE AUTHOR

Dr. Lance B. Eliot, MBA, PhD is the CEO of Techbruim, Inc. and Executive Director of the Cybernetic AI Self-Driving Car Institute and has over twenty years of industry experience including serving as a corporate officer in a billion dollar firm and was a partner in a major executive services firm. He is also a serial entrepreneur having founded, ran, and sold several high-tech related businesses. He previously hosted the popular radio show *Technotrends* that was also available on American Airlines flights via their in-flight audio program. Author or co-author of a dozen books and over 400 articles, he has made appearances on CNN, and has been a frequent speaker at industry conferences.

A former professor at the University of Southern California (USC), he founded and led an innovative research lab on Artificial Intelligence in Business. Known as the "AI Insider" his writings on AI advances and trends has been widely read and cited. He also previously served on the faculty of the University of California Los Angeles (UCLA), and was a visiting professor at other major universities. He was elected to the International Board of the Society for Information Management (SIM), a prestigious association of over 3,000 high-tech executives worldwide.

He has performed extensive community service, including serving as Senior Science Adviser to the Vice Chair of the Congressional Committee on Science & Technology. He has served on the Board of the OC Science & Engineering Fair (OCSEF), where he is also has been a Grand Sweepstakes judge, and likewise served as a judge for the Intel International SEF (ISEF). He served as the Vice Chair of the Association for Computing Machinery (ACM) Chapter, a prestigious association of computer scientists. Dr. Eliot has been a shark tank judge for the USC Mark Stevens Center for Innovation on start-up pitch competitions, and served as a mentor for several incubators and accelerators in Silicon Valley and Silicon Beach. He served on several Boards and Committees at USC, including having served on the Marshall Alumni Association (MAA) Board in Southern California.

Dr. Eliot holds a PhD from USC, MBA, and Bachelor's in Computer Science, and earned the CDP, CCP, CSP, CDE, and CISA certifications. Born and raised in Southern California, and having traveled and lived internationally, he enjoys scuba diving, surfing, and sailing.

ADDENDUM

AI Self-Driving Cars Autonomy

Practical Advances in Artificial Intelligence (AI) and Machine Learning

By

Dr. Lance B. Eliot, MBA, PhD

———

For supplemental materials of this book, visit:

www.ai-selfdriving-cars.guru

For special orders of this book, contact:

LBE Press Publishing

Email: LBE.Press.Publishing@gmail.com